Building
the
2020 Digital Team

Also by Michael de Kare-Silver:

Digital Insights 2020
e-Shock
Strategy in Crisis
Stre@mlining

Building
the
2020 Digital Team

How to Organise and Structure
for a Digital, Multi-Channel World

Michael de Kare-Silver

Matador
9 Priory Business Park,
Wistow Road, Kibworth Beauchamp,
Leicestershire. LE8 0RX
Tel: 0116 279 2299
Email: books@troubador.co.uk
Web: www.troubador.co.uk/matador
Twitter: @matadorbooks

ISBN 978 1785891 625

British Library Cataloguing in Publication Data.
A catalogue record for this book is available from the British Library.

Printed and bound by CPI Group (UK) Ltd, Croydon, CR0 4YY
Typeset in 11pt Aldine401 BT by Troubador Publishing Ltd, Leicester, UK

Matador is an imprint of Troubador Publishing Ltd

This is dedicated to my two best life friends: Alexander and Deborah

Contents

Chapter 1

Building the Digital Team

Why are some companies being especially successful in this digital world? How did children's wear retailer Zulily.com grow from zero to more than $1bn in revenues in less than 5 years, Kraft's Nabisco launch a new product line which achieved $100m of sales in 1 year, RELX Group migrate from being a print publisher to a highly regarded digital information software business, Barclays Bank forge ahead of its rivals as a "digital first" innovator, Amazon achieve its extraordinary market sector penetration and customer engagement? What are these types of companies doing to exploit the new, still fast-changing digital landscape and achieve that winning 2020 market position?

The answer lies in how they organise for digital, how they build their teams and their skills sets, how they develop a culture inside that is supportive and encouraging of digital innovation and development, how they share and learn, how they attract and retain key talent who can make the difference. They've got Digital into their mainstream, into their DNA, they realise its importance but most critically they act and behave and implement and deliver and reward for digital initiative and success.

There are 6 key decisions that need to get made if a company is to join these digital winners. These are around:

1. *Structure and Organisation*
2. *Leadership and Engine room*
3. *Skills and Scale*
4. *Culture and Style*
5. *Learning and Sharing*
6. *Talent Finding and Retaining*

Let's look at each in turn. Before we do it's worth reminding of the Facebook mantra that is written large on the walls of their office: "The journey is 1% finished". Facebook recognise and appreciate that "we've only just begun in our ambitions and what can be achieved". And it is a journey, not just for Facebook, but for all companies. The technology landscape continues to change at breath-taking speed, it's hard for any individual or company to keep up, the boundaries of what's possible and what is not keep changing, the potential for disruption in the market is never-ending, new possibilities and potential in existing and in new markets are surfacing all the time. This "technology revolution" that we are living through is still in its early stages. And just as the market place keeps evolving, so the journey for companies stretches out into time as an organisation tries to assimilate and absorb and process what all these changes may mean for its future, for what to invest in, what to prioritise, what skills and organisation shape and what technology changes required to capture these market opportunities and deliver continued shareholder value.

Many companies struggle with all the change opportunities, want to leapfrog and jump to some higher technical plane, but while that ambition may be laudable, it needs to come with the recognition that it does all take time. Leapfrogging for an established corporation is hard to do, in fact it's difficult for any company to make successful changes and even step-changes in the way it operates. So what's critical is, yes have the ambition for sure, have the clear goals and sense of mission and purpose. But put that into the context of what can the organisation cope with, how ready is it for change, what external catalysts and support and hiring is required to enable and facilitates these changes, what's the right timeframe and timetable that allows for the current business operations to keep going and developing even while new ways of working and new levels of customer engagement take shape and can begin to make their impact.

1. Structure and Organisation

A common question is: should we keep Digital as a separate stand-alone team and group or should we simply have it all somehow integrated into the core of the company?

Digital started off in every organisation as a separate group and team. There were these specialist skills such as Search engine optimisation, SEO and SEM, and such people were often pioneers, evangelists, sometimes technical geeks who did things and seemed to know things that others in the company barely understood but had been convinced were nevertheless somehow important for their customers. And of course, that "specialist" digital unit started to grow adding other skills such as "front end web developers", content writers, web designers, email marketers, web analysts… Over a short space of time a few specialists, at least in the larger organisations became a large team. And what's more, instead of just managing a bit of online brochureware, they were starting to drive ever larger chunks of revenue. Suddenly this team became the growth engine of the company.

At retailer John Lewis for example, so specialist and important did this team become, that they had their own offices in a separate building with its own team managers, culture, ways of working and doing its own thing, a mystery and black box to the rest of the organisation, more than 150 people, somehow though justifying themselves as they drew more and more plaudits from commentators and customers and became responsible for a sizeable percentage of the JL business.

For JL, there came a point where this mystery had gone on too long. There was a felt need to learn, to absorb, to transfer this customer and market know-how and get the whole organisation on-board with this way of thinking and engaging with customers. So the separate office was shut, the digital team was brought back into the head office, front end developers were reconnected with the IT team, online marketers were made a part of the wider company Marketing team, people were integrated. But still not completely. There is still a Head of Online and Digital who manages eg the specialist online marketers. That Head of Online may report to the equivalent of the CMO, but the digital team have still kept their distinctiveness and the organisation is forced to acknowledge that however much it may desire complete integration, that that goal today is just not possible, that there is need for specialists with particular skills and expertise. Yes make sure what they do is part of the overall long term customer vision and plan, but accept too that they need to move and innovate and operate often in a distinctive style and way and need to be given the scope to test and trial new market place ideas all the time.

This John Lewis vignette is mirrored in many other companies today. Should we leave the specialists to get on with it, or, if we "bring them back in", then will we lose that expertise and dilute the market potential? On the other hand, doesn't the whole organisation need to be working to an integrated multi-channel agenda? Shouldn't everyone be somehow involved now in this tech-led world?

To answer this question, it's critical to acknowledge and respect that each and every organisation is different. Every company is at different stages of its digital journey. If Facebook feel they are only at 1% then where are the long established corporations? Are the likes of eg GE or Philips or Procter & Gamble still only at the starting gate? Or has each in its own way in fact been effectively laying the foundations and building the capabilities that will enable it to succeed in a digital world? Each company has different culture, style and ways of thinking, each is at its own state of digital maturity and readiness and that as much as anything will determine and define how it organises and how it evolves, what it keeps specialist and what it integrates. But for most every company, the vision of a fully integrated, "we are all now digital" environment and organisation structure is still a long way off.

To help understand how any one particular organisation should structure its digital teams, the following sections can add perspective on how others are doing it and what needs to be considered in making the decision.

2. Leadership and Engine Room

Who should lead the Digital charge? It's now become so critical to so many companies' futures, that it has become a c-suite role. We now see an ever-growing number of "Chief Digital Officers" being appointed. This can reflect the growing recognition of just how much of the company's business is now dependent on being successful in this space.

This "elevation" of digital to the senior ranks has at the same time brought a number of tensions, especially in the relationship of the CDO with the CMO and CIO (too many "c's"?).

For example, who is responsible for the customer? Historically that responsibility would naturally have been the remit of the CMO. But if there is a CDO and eg half the revenues are online, then shouldn't perhaps the CDO have equal responsibility? And if so how does that "responsibility" get shared, who makes the final call?

This can get even more complicated where online becomes the majority of the business. If the CDO has P&L responsibility and is acknowledged as being the leader of that, then why is there a need for a separate group CEO, shouldn't the CDO in effect become the CEO?

All this is just a further illustration of the still relative immaturity of digital, or put another way, it's an example of where most companies are on their journey that this sort of issue is only just beginning to surface and has not yet been answered or addressed.

While this leadership battle rages away, there is also a next level challenge in the engine room. That is how best to organise and structure the digital teams, the key junior execs and mid-level managers who are building and driving and nurturing the business day by day. Part of this question is also where best to locate them. Is it a John Lewis type solution, should they remain separate, should they be integrated and if integrated then just how much!

One way of resolving this is to look at 3 companies who have each adopted a similar structures. The 3 are Amazon.com, Whitbread (Costa Coffee and Premier Inn) and Next, the clothing retail group.

Each of these vanguard companies has realised how important it is to get its web sites and online presence optimised. They have realised that this is not a once-a-year review, but needs to be something continuous and ongoing, ideally 24/7 and if possible in real time.

Each has responded to this challenge by restructuring and reorganising 3 specific teams. That is (i) the front end web developers, (ii) the web analytics and insight group and (iii) the online marketing team. The decision was made that these 3 groups be brought together, be co-located and sat next to each other and also report into the same person. Usually that's the Marketing Director or could be the Head of Site Optimisation or in other companies even the Chief Customer Officer.

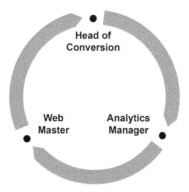

The web analytics team are constantly monitoring user journeys, fall out rates, which promotional offers are working and which are not, should a promotion be ended now, should the price be reduced or raised, should a call to action be made more prominent, put in a different colour, put in a different place on the web site, what's being said about the company, the products on social media, is any response needed, what else is happening externally with the weather, politics, sport, internationally that might influence or change what might work today, this hour, this minute online that could optimise the customer experience and maximise sales.

The web analytics team are identifying these change opportunities in real time, they share that with the Marketing /Commercial team who are charged with making immediate decisions on what to change if anything in response to the observed insights.

The front end web dev team then take over and make the changes, fast.

All this delivers a highly responsive, targeted, customised, digital operations environment that is looking at all that's going on, on desktop and mobile, and fine-tuning with agility and speed.

It is that type of "engine room" management and structuring that can make a tremendous difference to a company's success.

3. Skills and Scale

A significant challenge is how to afford the wide variety of specialists required to deliver the Digital potential. There seem to be any number of very distinct skill sets ranging through the value chain from Customer Awareness development through Customer Engagement and Conversion and then keeping them coming back!

The skills need necessarily to include some or all of SEO, SEM, online media display, affiliates, content, social media, creative design, conversion, analytics, e-commerce /transaction management, CRM, fulfilment, returns, technical web development, project management, mobile, partnerships and intermediaries, product /service strategy, roadmap and innovation…

Some companies just don't have the size and scale of budgets to afford to bring in specialists for each one of these areas. Many other companies do have the scale and budget potential but have other priorities or just don't appreciate and realise the need and value potential or have other pressures on costs and people.

The typical compromise is to bring in a few and ask them to multi-task, to work across the whole digital value chain and do their best to optimise where possible. Such an approach may be a fiscal necessity but it's important that an organisation does appreciate what skills it does *not* have and so adjusts its targets and expectations accordingly.

For some others, the solution involves bringing in contractors and freelancers for a particular project only and justifying that resource on the back of a specific project RoI. That can work well though clearly individuals hired on that temporary basis will sometimes lack the emotional engagement with the product and brand and the genuine desire and passion to go the extra mile to make this succeed.

An alternative solution is to set up a network of support agencies and consultancies who can advise and take on specific projects eg rebuild the web site.

Whatever the solution path that is chosen, it should be part of a long term strategy that looks at the role digital can play in an organisation and looks at a gradual build up in budgets and people and capabilities. Only taking a purely year by year approach that is at best incremental and will perhaps squeeze a 5% increase in spend and activity - such an approach is unlikely to match the pace of change in the company's market place and the readiness of customers to embrace any digital initiatives the company does make.

B2B companies have been especially "guilty" of this slow incremental approach, looking at the slow pace of their competitors and using that to justify their own inactivity. But many such organisations have found that if they do invest and create an effective digital marketplace for their customers then it can have a significant impact and gets a surprisingly quick and positive customer response. Companies like Cisco, Intel, BP, Coats, BT, Pitney Bowes have all discovered that if they do divert resources and spend to Digital then *it does pay back.*

4. Culture and Style

Successful digital-led companies have developed 3 core elements to their culture:

- fostering an entrepreneurial spirit
- creating an agile environment of "test, trial and learn"
- recognising that we are going through an era of fast change and that there will be ambiguity and uncertainty and that that is ok!

The best digital people are often pioneers, they thrive on change, they look for adventure and the chance to explore possibilities, they aren't comfortable working in an environment where everything is set, where there's little room for manoeuver, they want to work fast and get things done, and not wait 6 months for IT to change some copy on the web site. They are more instinctively entrepreneurs, they thrive where that spirit is fostered and supported, they are comfortable with change and actually are prepared to push for that, ambiguity does not unsettle or discomfort them, on the contrary that is what they expect and what enables them to think and act and come up with disruptive solutions that can be game-changers.

In today's world, a winning business needs these sort of people in its midst. Such individuals can also help shift the whole corporate culture to a more focussed 21st century business model.

5. Learning and Sharing

Hyper Island is one of the world's leading learning and training centres for Digital. Its 3 day "Digital Masterclass" is almost legendary in its ability to convert doubting or uncertain execs into overnight digital evangelists. It's set up for groups of senior execs but can also be used at all levels across the company. There are usually around 30 in the class group and it's a full 3 day immersion, staying overnight, working hard in both lectures and workshops and presentations that share what others are achieving and driving out what could be possible.

Less a "class" than an introduction to a new way of thinking, it's intended as an intensive immersion and learning and there are other groups that do this as well including the major business schools like MIT, Columbia and INSEAD but the Hyper Island can appeal as it's more "short sharp e-shock".

There are also any number of seminars and conferences that seek to train and share best practices and latest ideas eg at the IDM (Institute of Direct Marketing) and at CIM (Chartered Institute of Marketing). For those who want to dig deeper there are longer training programmes such as the MSc (a part time /evenings /remote learning programme) in Internet Retailing at Manchester Metropolitan University and coordinated by e-Consultancy.

These courses do not just appeal to those who wish to learn. They also have a pivotal role where a group of execs in a company are trying to drive through digital change and technology innovation and encountering resistance and hesitation from colleagues whose support they need. If such colleagues can be persuaded to participate in some external education and enlightenment, then it can of course change the pace and direction of the company's development and investment.

This need for immersion, learning and training, for sharing ideas and expertise is all the more critical in the digital world. Things are moving fast, they are changing, new more agile start-up ventures are springing up out of nowhere challenging incumbents and disrupting decades long and traditional ways of thinking and operating. Innovations may be customer-facing but they can also be internal process-driven enabling eg lower costs of production or automating processes which can speed up time to market. It's near impossible to do the day job and stay up-to-date on all the potential disruptive forces at work, so sharing, training, listening to experts, finding, somehow, that occasional time to listen and learn, creating the environment at work which both encourages and enables that, that can all lay the foundations for a successful future.

6. Talent Finding and Retaining

Many say that they find it very difficult to attract key digital talent. They may find it takes months, perhaps even 6 to 9 months to find someone. In some cases, companies give up on that targeted hire altogether. They either make do, or have to reach out to some agency or consultancy to provide the resource and support.

Yet some companies have it seems no problem at all in quickly attracting the right sort of candidate profile. Whether it's a start-up like Zulily.com, a complex audit /advisory group like Deloitte, a B2B publisher like Incisive, manufacturer distributors like Huawei, Smith & Nephew and Brady or the likes of Tesco and Argos.

How do companies develop that talent attraction? The 7 simple keys are:

i.   A good quality online presence so that when the candidate looks up the company for the first time they get a good impression,
ii. A good "digital story", a good explanation available as to where the company is on its digital journey, a recognition that there is a long way still to go, a sense of that adventure and what the goals are,
iii. A commitment to digital from the CEO and through-out the corporation,
iv. A readiness to invest, even modestly, in new ideas
v.   A fast-paced interview process that takes weeks not months
vi. A reasonable amount of flexibility around the job spec so as not to exclude

good, bright, fast-learning people who may not be able to tick all the boxes yet on the spec.

vii. Flexibility, within reason, on pay and benefits.

Sometimes it may just eg need a small sign-on to compensate an exec for loss of bonus accrued at previous employ or need to buy a season ticket for the longer commute.

It just requires a readiness and desire to move quickly, be flexible and make it easy for the right candidates to say yes!

Another way of thinking about this is to reflect on the prospective employee "user journey". There's lots of talk and effort going into to the optimisation of the customer journey to maximise conversion. Much less attention has been paid to the *employee* experience and how that can be optimised to streamline hiring and make acceptance easy.

From the first contact to the last and then through to the on-boarding process, who in the company is responsible? HR initiate and coordinate but they require the hiring managers to do their bit and make time available, not cancel interviews at the last minute, give immediate feedback, be prepared properly for the interviews, recognise that for the candidate this can be a life-changing moment and so treat that moment with the respect it deserves.

Too often, even for relatively junior roles, there can be 6 to 12 interviews (in one case I know of 24!). It is of course almost impossible that a candidate will be liked by everyone they see. Does one "no" outweigh 9 "yes's"? That can often be the case. And as each interview is set up, so the timetable is drawn out, the weeks turn into months and meantime a faster-moving company comes in and snaps up the prospective hire.

Getting this right helps get the right candidate on board. But then they also need to be retained. Good digital people are on every recruiter's radar screen. They may just have moved jobs but they're still getting calls about new opportunities. So if the new job does not live up to expectations they can be seduced and intrigued by something elsewhere, "the grass is greener?"

★★★★★

By way of a summary, we can review the following Barclays case study, looking at how the Bank has become more "digital first".

From CEO Ashok Vaswani came a stream of communications about digital. His mantra: "Digitization is redefining and transforming our business".

This has included a wide number of initiatives. The target has been to educate the workforce and turn each and every employee into a digital evangelist. And through that galvanise and engage customers in a more digital-designed way. Vaswani's goal was for employees to become more digitally literate, to bring about new ways to connect with customers, to identify new business and revenue streams and to take advantage of new technologies.

Internally, people were encouraged to dress more comfortably, the work space was changed to include pods and chill-out areas, football tables appeared!, ties disappeared, seminars were held with the idea of teaching everyone about why digital is important and what that would mean.

Employees were encouraged to become "digital natives" and to participate in various training programmes inside the bank and externally too. "Reverse mentors" were set up, throughout the bank, so that senior execs were deliberately exposed to latest digital ideas and diplomatically encouraged to change ways of operating. The Bank launched its high profile Digital Eagles consumer publicity campaign ensuring that each and every branch had its own digital champion who could encourage consumers to use the newly installed self-serve machines rather than stand in line and wait for counter service. 12000 Digital Eagles have so far been trained to evangelise at branch level. Alongside this, is the Barclays Digital Code Playground, a widely-advertised initiative to encourage people to come to "learn to code" training sessions run for free in the Bank's local branches.

What does all this mean? It starts to change a whole culture across a huge and sprawling organisation. The employees feel the need to be a part of this as it starts to become an accelerated route for promotion and higher bonus levels. It showcases the Bank in a different light to a perhaps cynical or sceptical public who begin to change their perception of what Barclays can do for them.

Banks are unlikely to ever have a warm cuddly brand image, they're not going to be like a Mothercare or Marks and Spencer, but they can move with the times, they can change what they stand for, they can use digital to streamline how they organise and operate, they can look for new ways of working that will make it easy for customers to use their services online and by mobile, they can create an environment where employees feel there is opportunity and adventure and that things are moving forward, they can help make themselves seen as the leading employer for digital servcies in the financial services sector, they can look to be a 21st century winner and leave other rivals behind.

Chapter 2

Does Investment in Digital Pay Back?

Given that Digital and new Tech agility has become so important, there's a key question to address: *does investment in Digital pay-back?* Is it a long term play building a platform for the future that may perhaps deliver 5 years out? Or can investment *now* deliver early wins and results?

There's significant pressure on companies these days to "get digital". This can range from hiring in a new "Chief Digital Officer" to re-launching e-Commerce, expanding social media, setting up advanced Analytics and data mining, automating for self-serve, generating new business leads online, even taking stakes in myriad start-ups…the list of potential opportunities is endless but what's it all worth?

For the first time there's now some reassurance that it *is* all worthwhile. It's not just about doing it because competitors are, or the brokers and analysts expect you to, or because the Marketing and Sales teams are saying you have to, there is now some strong proof and validation that it does truly result in increased profitability to the point of leading sector ROI.

This proof comes from the first truly rigorous piece of research. It was carried out by MIT. Published recently in the Harvard Business Review and also a book called Leading Digital. The top line shows that those who become "Digital Masters" are *26% more profitable* than their industry peers. Those who lag behind in this digital race are 24% less profitable.

It's an extraordinary finding and the research covers some 300 + companies across the world and across different industry sectors. Time and again the MIT team found these high levels of success repeated. So what's going on, what lies behind the research, what's it take to become a "Digital Master"?

To begin with the Research team found there were basically 4 types of companies. These could be categorised as Beginners, "Fashionistas", Conservatives and Digital Masters. And this categorisation was at its most stark when the comparison was done by different industry sector. So it was more likely to find Masters in Retail or Personal Banking. Whereas in B2B

Manufacturing, most organisations were well behind the digital curve, despite evidence that even in that sector, those who did invest did get results.

Four Levels of Digital Mastery

Digital Masters Outperform Their Peers

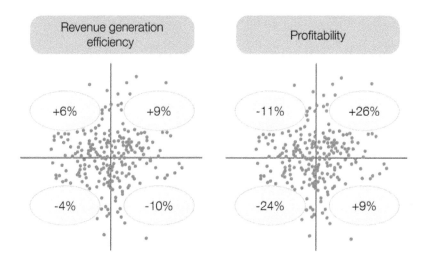

Digital Mastery by Industry

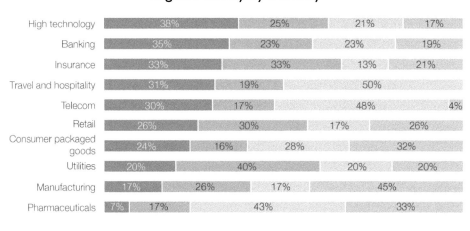

The MIT research has also highlighted what are the key success factors:
While it was for sure about the appetite to invest and the relative amount of investment, it was *also* about the execution and delivery. Some companies were shown to have invested in teams and technology platforms but the investment was kept siloed, the digital team stood on its own, it functioned more as a separate division, there was little integration with the core business, and so little change in the basic business processes and operations. That led to resentment on all sides, frustration in the digital team who were limited in what they could achieve and resentment in the core business who felt much needed investment funds were being diverted.

What led to success was to marry the digital strategy and investment, alongside also building the digital transformation capability *inside* the core business. The research shows that it was essential to develop the change and implementation leadership skills, to ramp up the PMO team, to identify the core projects and staff them up with leadership and change delivery expertise, that what helped was having a core Steering Committee, led by the CEO, that held weekly or monthly reviews, in-depth, around the change agenda, milestones and progress, so that everyone saw this was a top CEO item and needed the attention and priority to make things happen.

Case Study: Asian Paints is one of these "Digital Masters". They are India's largest paint company and operate across Asia with revenues of c. $2bn. The CIO there Manish Choksi attributes their success to "successive waves of digital transformation".

Their aim has been to globalise, maintain high levels of growth (they have hit 15% cagr over past 15 yrs), and to do that while increasing efficiency, innovating and enhancing the customer experience through digital engagement and also important for them, to continue to reduce their environmental impact. "We are spread over 120 locations and deal directly with some thirty thousand retailers so getting our growth strategy right around digital is critical for us".

Among other things they have established a standard e-Commerce platform which all the operating subsidiaries must use, they have one unified and now centralised customer ordering process which is self-serve and online and standardised; the Sales team have embraced this online order process and have changed their role from order-takers to strategic advisors to existing customers while adding a key new business /new customer focus to their work and revenue targets. In addition, steps in the supply chain have been automated with new technology tools and workflow software wherever possible to reduce the level of manpower and error, and they have also taken advantage of new Cloud-based partner software to better manage relationships. There is now a more in-depth data and performance management capability and that has led to more insight around product profitability and led to the roll-out of a new premium product range to meet a new identified customer segment need. All-in-all a significant set of steps and as Manish Choksi acknowledges: "the road ahead continues with our ongoing digital transformation well into the future".

Case Study: Pages Jaunes (the French Yellow Pages) has unlike its UK and US counterparts been a real success. Its recent strong financial results announcement was headlined: "Success of Digital investment, acceleration of revenue growth".

Why did Pages Jaunes succeed while UK and US Yellow Pages effectively both went bankrupt?

CEO of Pages Jaunes Jean Pierre Remy is widely respected as the leader of that company's digital transformation.

For Jean Pierre Remy, the challenge was how to adapt from publishing a book to competing effectively with Google, Yelp, Craigslist and other local providers. The organisation challenge was difficult as many remained sceptical about digital and were reluctant to abandon old ways of working and embrace new technology tools. Nevertheless Remy went ahead and detailed his vision that within 5 years they would move to a "75% digital business".

A lot of time was spent across the whole workforce explaining what this meant and the urgent need to do something. In many ways the digital vision and the need to embrace it was reinforced by continuing declining revenues from the old traditional book business.

To address this opportunity, Remy also realised he needed an injection of new people with developed digital and new technology skills, people who were adept at business transformation and who could lead the charge. In addition there was a substantial re-training programme put in place educating about digital, new ways of working and what each person could do to contribute to that.

Over the following two or three years, Pages Jaunes established a new agile / test-trial-learn culture which led to rapid development of prototypes at low cost to test out ideas and applications, an early commitment to mobile anticipating the rush to smart phone access to the Net, a joint venture partnership with Google which became a key way of turning a formidable competitor into a marketing and technology ally, a 100% switch of all capex and opex into a "digital first" strategy deliberately winding down the book business, and regular 2-weekly presentations to the Board Operating Committee updating on all the key digital transformation work streams, identifying roadblocks and getting immediate go /no-go decisions. It's all worked, as shown in the table here below:

Pages Jaunes Metrics Table

Evolution of Internet fixed and mobile audiences for 4ᵗʰ quarter

In millions of visits	Latest Yr	Previous Yr	Change
PagesJaunes	387.7	340.8	+13.7%
of which mobile	129.0	100.9	+27.8
Mappy	79.0	69.2	+14.2%
of which mobile	32.7	26.2	+24.9%
ComprendreChoisir	34.0	18.3	+85.1%
of which mobile	12.4	4.6	+170.3%
Other	24.8	28.5	-12.8%
Total*	525.5	456.9	+15.0%
of which mobile	179.0	135.5	+32.1%

Source: Solocal Group

In summary, the MIT Research team distilled what they found as the 4 key practices which marked out Asian Paints, Pages Jaunes, Unilever, Procter & Gamble, Seven Eleven Japan, EMC, Codelco, American Express, Burberry and a host of others as "Digital Masters". Those 4 key steps are:

1. *"Framing the digital challenge":* A unified consolidated CEO and Board decision that Digital is key to the company's future and the identification of the digital vision, targets and future state.

2. *"Focussing the investment"*: Putting in place the funding for the transformation
3. *"Mobilising the organisation"*: Communicating constantly, reinforcing the same set of messages and goals, using Social Media tools to encourage bottom-up ideation, sharing the rewards and upside as progress gets made.
4. *"Sustaining the transition"*: recognising this is not a one-off exercise, but the need to build a sustainable innovation and change culture, a culture that rewards change and does not condemn well-intentioned failure, an ability to measure progress both internally and externally vs. competition and ensuring a continuous programme of employee awareness-building, education and technical literacy.

The Digital Transformation Compass

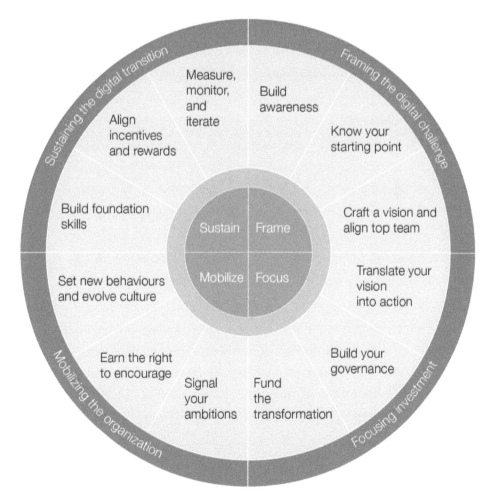

Source: MIT Center for Digital Business/Leading Digital

★★★★★

Becoming a "Digital Master" or put another way, leading a successful digital transformation of the company, was rated the biggest challenge facing all organisations no matter what the industry sector in a recent McKinsey study.

It's being able to reach beyond the short term earnings and profits targets and seeing the future 5 year picture and market state, it's being able to see what needs to change, about setting priorities and perhaps most critically somehow finding the funding and investment to enable the change and transformation to take place. At some companies, like Pages Jaunes, there was no choice, it was a do or die move and that helped galvanise the workforce and manage investor expectations of when they could expect a return. But where there's no crisis, as at Asian Paints, it required the Board and CEO to make a fundamental decision about how to succeed in the long term, a reappraisal of strategy, a review of all budget spend, a refocus of effort and activity, a stop on things that weren't clearly about a digital future, a readiness to leverage the balance sheet if necessary, a willingness to consider radical alliances or joint ventures, a desire to "test trial learn".

In the MIT research they suggest this first step for any organisation considering this major change: carry out an internal and confidential survey across the entire workforce and ask this question: *"how ready are we to succeed in the digital technology age?"*

Chapter 3

Chief Digital Officers

Who are They and Where to Find Them!

The previous chapter shows that effective investment in Digital *does pay back*. So how best go about capturing those benefits?

A number of companies are now looking to create the new role of Chief Digital Officer. According to a recent Gartner Research survey: "a CDO champion will become a "must-have expertise" in most every major company as we move toward 2020". And perhaps not surprisingly, there's been a surge of new CDO posts and jobs being established. Companies like Aviva, Visa, Lloyds Bank, GE, Bayer, even the BBC, have all rushed to do this. And often at very senior level and at the heart of the company. Why and what is this person supposed to be doing?

To some extent, the answer is clear and obvious. *"Digital is now so important to us we need senior level leadership", "our future growth depends on finding new digital revenue streams", "our shareholders expect us to be a Digital Leader".* And with the continued rapid pace of digital technology advancement, with consumers' continued and growing appetite for digital communications, and with ever-easier, more convenient, more secure ways to buy online, so the need for digital talent and skills to meet this demand grows apace.

But what does a CDO do? There's no proven role or job description here. It's new and each company is figuring out what works best for its organisation, its culture and its preferred ways of working. There are at least 3 different types of CDO out there!

1. Digital Champion: this type of CDO has no P&L responsibility but is more a "centre of excellence". The digital champion is intended to be the fount of digital knowledge, a gatherer of good ideas, a sharer of best practices, a challenger to others in the organisation, a voice at the exec committee meetings.

For some companies, this is a good and easy way to start, most others in the company can easily accept this sort of role and can take from it whatever they want, without worrying that it will ever really interfere with what they do or truly disrupt their day-to-day operations. For the CDO, it can be a voice of influence but can be a lonely position. It is likely they will have no or only a very small team of eg "digital strategists" and it can lead to frustration all-round once the novelty of the job has worn off. It can be a good signal to shareholders of future intent but is unlikely to materially change things.

2. Digital New Business MD: this type of CDO can make an impact. This person will typically have responsibility for identifying new digital-based business opportunities whether through organic growth, joint ventures or acquisition. They will be presenting the business case to the Board, agreeing the investment and then taking responsibility for building the operating team to make it happen. For that they will have formal P&L and investment accountability. It's clearly a role that has teeth!

Companies like Barclaycard, Sainsbury's, HomeServe, Unilever and others have all variously moved down this path. In some cases the role is called CEO or MD Digital, in other cases it might be MD New Ventures or even more plainly Business Development Director but the thrust is the same: explore this digital world, leverage our assets and our Brand(s), see what digital innovation can achieve.

Where this sort of CDO is established it's because the business leaders of the company want to be innovative and brave. They appreciate that doing things quickly within existing legacy systems, structures and processes will take time, and that the digital world is moving at a faster pace. So why not for example allow this CDO to set up new venture(s), give them the freedom of their own space, team, culture and technology, give them some headroom to move with agility and flexibility and see what that can generate. At minimum the organisation can learn about new digital ways of working and new tech solutions that can achieve in a few weeks what the legacy environment would achieve only after some many months of complexity. At best, it will spawn new businesses and new revenue opportunities that can drive total growth and potentially become part of the company's future.

3. Business Transformation Director. This type of CDO role is the toughest. But in some ways also the most essential. While a CDO as digital champion can be a bit of fun and makes the symbolic gesture, while the Digital MD might be very productive but still sits outside the core business, this type of CDO strikes at the very heart of the company. It's what all companies need but most in various ways pay lip-service to, rather than grasp at it eagerly and make it part of their core agenda.

It's because Digital is not only about new ways of connecting to customers. It's also of course about new ways of working, new opportunities to automate internal processes, technical innovations that can streamline and accelerate how long it takes to get something done, that can get new products to market quicker and with more impact. It cuts root and branch into the guts of the organisation. It affects all and every department. It challenges historic ways of working. It's not an easy role. Any CDO attempting fundamental change will come up against all the classic change obstacles: *"it's just not possible"*, *"we tried that and it doesn't work"*, *"customers won't like it"*, *"it's not a priority right now"," it will jeopardise our business", "it will mean we won't be able to make budget this year"*…etc.

So this type of CDO needs the heartfelt and deep commitment from the rest of the Board and from the CEO especially to empower and enable the role to be effective. Being a "digital champion" and evangelist is all very well, but this role needs to be more of a "collaborator", a listener, an outstanding stakeholder manager, someone who can adeptly prioritise, get some early wins, pick the "low-hanging" fruit and gradually build up a groundswell and momentum for digital change.

Ultimately, it is only those companies who do embark on this kind of digital change programme who will be able to take advantage of the new digital world and there are already many examples of companies who have missed the digital change boat. With Kodak the most obvious, but with a number of retail and media companies especially who are struggling while watching the likes of Amazon, eBay, Expedia, Netflix and Apple Pay eat their lunch!

★★★★★

Once an organisation has decided to appoint a CDO and worked out the best "type" that will fit into their digital journey, then the next question is where can these people best be found, what's the talent pool like, how much do they cost, what sort of skills and backgrounds will best work?

A recent survey by the CDO Club of New York found CDO roles in many countries across the world. The US and the UK were at the forefront of this new role development reflecting the highly developed digital economy in both countries. Australia, Finland and Singapore were other countries also seeing a lot of initiative and activity in this area. But there are early pioneering CDOs from Brazil to Czech Republic to New Zealand. So this is very definitely a growing global trend which is expected to accelerate.

The CDO Club survey also showed that most of those appointed come from a commercial rather than technical background, i.e with a Marketing / Sales /Business Development orientation. This is perhaps surprising when most everything to do with digital has technology at its heart. In fact in the early days of "new media" and "interactive" it was often the IT department who had claimed ownership for digital as they turned some of their software development team into front-end web developers building the early web sites.

Since those early pioneering days, it has become increasingly clear that while the technology is key, it's the exploitation of that technology that most companies are desperate for and the need to convert the technical into the commercial. While there is absolutely no doubt that a good IT Director can take on that broader commercial /business development opportunity, most of the job specs for CDOs today being prepared by HR teams will focus on the commercialisation of digital and indicate a preference for the Sales /Marketing background and skill set. There are very good Tech leaders who can justifiably challenge that but it is where most CDOs appointments are focussed.

What's the size of the talent pool? The answer is that it is relatively limited. While there are many with eg 10 yrs experience and are expert eg in Search or eCRM or Social Media, there are far fewer with the depth of experience, the maturity, the senior stakeholder management skills who can sit confidently and comfortably at Board /c-Level and engage effectively around digital change opportunities.

So the talent pool, especially for the "type 3" CDO as Business Transformation Leader, is harder to find and yet inevitably in high demand.

It means HR teams may need to think creatively and laterally about the sort of person and background that can do these CDO jobs, be open to consider strong technology leaders with an aptitude for the commercial, be ready to consider eg those from a Consulting background as opposed to only those from major corporate line-management roles, be ready to acknowledge that however important digital depth is to the role, that the other key job spec attributes are just as critical and eg change skills may ultimately be more important.

How much do they cost? High demand, small genuinely qualified talent pool can only result in pressure on remuneration levels. Even a year ago in the UK, a sensible target base salary band would have been c. £125k to £175k. But this has without doubt now gone up another notch and base salaries around the £200k + mark are not uncommon. Indeed in my research, I have found several at around £300k and a few in New York at $1m plus!

What is also happening here is that many digital experts are also very entrepreneurial so there may be flexibility in the way the remuneration is structured. It means many will have an intuitive interest in lower base /higher upside for achieving success. That doesn't work for those companies where there are fixed wage /pay structures and salary bands. But this is another area that the new digital world is challenging. If digital is key, if potentially so much of the company's future hinges on digital success, if this role is expected to drive fundamental change and innovation, then maybe "legacy" pay structures need also to be challenged and made more flexible?

★★★★★

What all commentators and practitioners do agree is that we are in the midst of a business revolution, that digital technology is changing what is possible, that new agile start-ups are quickly seizing market share and opening up new business opportunities, and so established companies must respond, there is no longer any choice, it's not even a question of when to grasp the challenge, it's an acknowledged immediate imperative and the only question now is how best to do it and who to hire to lead the charge!

Chapter 4

Chief Customer Officers

Some companies are adopting an alternative approach to capturing the Digital upsides. With digital pushing out the multi-channel boundaries, there's been renewed interest in hiring "Chief Customer Officers". Companies as diverse as Tesco, Philips, Apple, SAP and AllState Insurance have all appointed Chief Customer Officers, or people with equivalent job titles (eg at Apple, Angela Ahrendts, the former Burberry CEO, is called the Chief Customer Experience Officer).

These are senior roles, their aim is clearly to make the company more customer-centric and put that more firmly at the heart of the business. But what's caused this heightened sensitivity and commitment to customers? Surely companies have been advised and guided from time immemorial to be customer-centric, get close to their customers, understand and even anticipate customer needs. Most every company already has some kind of process and tools and resources that are aimed at meeting these customer goals. Organisations like Procter & Gamble and Coca-Cola have huge customer marketing departments and spend many millions of $, yet they have found value in appointing CCOs. Is there now then some realisation that existing ways of connecting with customers are inadequate, that today's customers need something more and that companies are struggling to work out what that "more" might be? Surely companies like Apple today are already proven in the customer engagement stakes, why lure the CEO from Burberry, what more can Angela Ahrendts, however skilled she might be, bring to this agenda?

The key here is digital. The advent of digital communication has been to empower the customer. Customers have more choices, have more information, expect more personalised messaging and marketing, want things now, have greater expectation that brands, companies, suppliers will deliver what they want and when they want it, not at the company's convenience, but at theirs. And digital technology has enabled new start-ups, disrupters, new agile, fast moving competitors to quickly enter a market sector and establish rapid awareness and market penetration. Social media and viral messaging can create an overnight winner. It's a customer revolution and companies have been struggling to catch-up with this fast pace of change and development. So leaving it to existing teams, processes and ways of working is proving too slow and ponderous. The need is to find other ways to make the necessary leap-forward in customer engagement.

Compounding this is the fragmentation of communication and marketing channels and the urgent need for an organisation to understand all the different ways that customers are interacting with them. It can be through social media or direct mail or online e-commerce or email or call centre or through a Sales rep or via a promotion in a magazine, at a trade-show, at a conference or through a TV or radio ad, through the mobile phone…it can be one of these contact routes or through a combination and how possibly understand that mix of customer engagement channels, which are more important, which work best, which mix of channels deliver the best customer engagement, what should be the priorities and focus?

Getting a complete view of the customer is increasingly important. The customer wants that too. If they've just purchased online then why doesn't the call centre know that? If they've responded by direct mail in the past then why aren't their details already registered for them to buy again online? Why doesn't the company have a complete "single view" of them so that future marketing and engagement can be optimised and delivered most efficiently?

It's into these sort of challenges that a Chief Customer Officer is hired. Their key is to understand that total customer experience and ensure it is as streamlined and as effective and as satisfying to the customer as possible.

Let's look at some case studies:

Electrolux (Appliance Manufacturer) had historically been Product / Manufacturing-led and was organised in different product teams with their own P&Ls and silo mentality. For customers this meant there was no joined-up consistent single view of Electrolux, its product range and its marketing. Customer research showed that the company was poorly perceived and the overall customer experience was lowly rated. This had been made worse because digital channels had inevitably led to more media and comms fragmentation compounding the number of different ways Electrolux went to market.

Eventually, MaryKay Kopf, the CMO, took Board responsibility for Customer Experience and led a full review of the whole customer experience area. The key decision was made to bring digital, brand, trade and product teams together to create a cohesive customer view from pre-purchase through to after sales and service. This new grouping was called, simply, the Customer Experience team. Supporting it was a new alignment around R&D, Manufacturing and IT to ensure the "back office" was in sync with the front and it was possible to consider a full end-to-end customer experience value chain.

To enable this whole re-organisation, there were cross-functional teams established to force through sharing and collaboration and the organisation institutionalised a key customer satisfaction metric as a core KPI which was factored into everyone's bonus plan.

The result has seen nine consecutive quarters of organic growth, a significant increase in the number of new product innovations brought to market and an increase in the speed of that happening. In addition, in terms of that core customer satisfaction KPI, Electrolux moved from near the bottom of the list to close to the top, beating out many rivals.

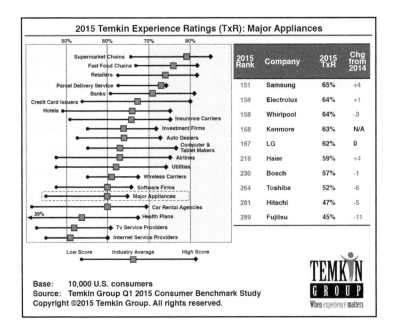

House of Fraser has been on a journey to provide a joined-up and consistent customer experience for a number of years, building what it calls "a seamless multi-channel operation". The whole initiative is led by Andy Harding. He was initially the Director of Digital, then became Director of Multi-Channel as House of Fraser began to develop the integrated cross-channel customer engagement. More recently, Andy's job title has changed again to Chief Customer Officer as he champions the customer throughout the organisation.

With his team, Andy is the voice of the customer at every level of the company and every conversation is about how best continue to develop so that the customer genuinely enjoys the same experience no matter whether they engage in-store or via desktop or mobile or call centre.

As a result, House of Fraser is ranked in the top 5 of Multi-Channel Retailers by Internet Retailing surveys, is leading in providing in-store online access for staff and customers to the company's total product range, has enabled inventory visibility and transparency across all customer and staff touchpoints, is able therefore to initiate immediate delivery ordering, has a growing click collect service as well as click pick-up from store or local coffee shop through partnership with Café Nero and is constantly innovating in terms of mobile /tablet payment solutions. "Of course no-one can accurately predict how technologies will evolve, but because we have been investing in making this customer experience a success, we are very well-placed to take continuing advantage of new innovations and developments".

★★★★★

Another key factor driving this "focus on the customer" has been the emergence of Net Promoter Score ("NPS"). This is a simple scoring on how well a company is delivering on customer service. It's a system pioneered by Bain Consulting and Satmetrix. The power lies in monitoring and measuring the NPS trend, but also in being able to benchmark versus competition. In addition Satmetrix publishes quarterly statistics which publicise which companies are improving their NPS and which ones are lagging. So even if a company is not formally evaluating its NPS it can become potentially publicly embarrassed to be part of a PR headline describing winners and losers in customer effectiveness. The whole NPS /Satmetrix system has only been running for a few years but it has quickly become a key performance indicator and is also looked at as a shareholder value indicator by prospective investors.

With all that going on it may become less of an optional extra and more of a necessary tool in governing the company.

NPS relies on one simple question: *"How likely is that you would recommend this company to a friend or colleague?"*. Customers respond on a 0 to 10 point rating with the view that a score of 6 or less means customers *"are unhappy and risk damaging your Brand and impeding growth through negative word of mouth"*. There's no ambiguity there!

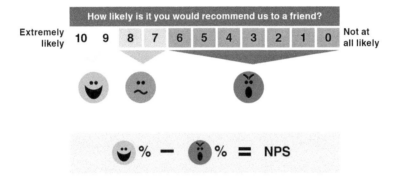

The NPS advocates talk about the scoring being only just the start. It's intended to be a catalyst to a complete review of the company's performance and the identification of a series of change and improvement initiatives to address any bad scores (cue for the consultant firms who have signed up as NPS "partners" themselves to explain how they can help!).

A recent NPS report was illustrative of the impact that this public benchmarking can have. Headlines appeared such as:

"Royal Bank of Scotland has the lowest customer loyalty scores of all the companies analysed."

"EE and Vodafone are bottom for Mobile and Internet Services. EE scored -7 for Mobile and -17 for Internet, Vodafone scored -1 and -18."

"Tesco is winning back customers' loyalty with eg its Tesco credit card scoring +23, beaten only by Santander at +28."

"Apple retains its title as customer loyalty champions with the top score again of all companies surveyed at +69"

The results are drawn from ongoing surveys of 11,000 UK Consumers. In the USA, the survey panel now reaches 80,000 consumers, all on a quarterly basis.

Another organisation has also entered this field called the National Consumer Satisfaction Index ("NCSI"). They seek to provide similar benchmarks to NPS, and to gain their own notoriety they publish scores by company by industry sector, with more detailed commentaries and reports that can be paid for.

An example from one of their previous Retail Banking reports (their scoring is simply out of 100):

Retail Banks

	Base-line	09	10	11	12	13	14	Previous Year % Change	First Year % Change
All Others	79	76	75	75	81	78	80	3.0	1.0
Santander	64	63	68	69	70	72	80	11.0	25.0
Lloyds Banking Group					74	73	77	5.0	4.0
Retail Banks^	**71**	**70**	**71**	**72**	**74**	**74**	**76**	**3.0**	**7.0**
HSBC	71	70	78	74	75	78	76	3.0	7.0
Barclays	68	69	70	72	73	74	74	0.0	9.0
RBS Group	71	69	68	72	72	71	71	0.0	0.0
HBOS	67	68	66	69	#	#	#	N/A	N/A
Lloyds TSB	70	69	70	73	#	#	#	N/A	

★★★★★

Jeanne Bliss, in her book titled "Chief Customer Officer", talks about a process for achieving a Customer-centric, customer-focussed organisation. Bliss held senior Customer Experience /Customer Loyalty management roles at Mazda, AllState and at Microsoft and has leveraged that know-how to identify the best process and techniques. The steps Bliss describes are reinforced by research from Gartner and the consultancy firm Prophet to provide a helpful framework and Bliss advocates finding measures and performance indicators to monitor and guide progress:

1. Honour and Manage Customer as Key Assets
    - *Measure customers gained and customers lost and care about.*

2. Align around experience
    - *Establish a company-wide responsibility for customer satisfaction. It's not just a Sales issue, it's not just up to any one department or team. The whole company should celebrate customer satisfaction and feel responsible for any customer disappointments.*

3. Build a customer listening path
    - *Set up key customer effectiveness surveys and ongoing research. Ensure all key execs interact with customers and check on the company's strengths and weaknesses.*

4. Map the customer journey
    - *Define the key steps of the different customer purchasing and interaction touch-points to identify areas of strength and weakness.*

5. Be Proactive
    - *Institutionalise these steps so that there is a developed and intimate knowledge of customers, how well the company is doing with them and importantly be able to anticipate their changing needs.*

6. Deliver one-company consistent and desired experiences
    - *Transform the systems and processes to cut away silo activity and deliver integrated customer planning and implementation*

7. Embrace Leadership behaviours which encourage Customer-centric priorities
    - *Develop the culture that unites leaders around integrated customer goals and actions.*

Recent research by Gartner showed that 89% of companies wanted to compete primarily around customer experience. This showed a significant shift away from previous core priorities which were typically around price or product.

Gartner concluded from its survey that much of this new customer emphasis was a result of "digital technology giving customers more access to information, more control of how and when and where they purchased, thus forcing companies to completely review their customer behaviour, traditional ways of customer engagement and revitalise their approach".

★★★★★

One last area to consider is where does this Chief Customer Officer sit in the organisation? The C-Suite is already crowded with everything from CIO and CTO to CMO and CPO as well as a CFO and CHRO, to name but a few!

Should companies add yet another person to the senior exec team? Some companies like NewsCorp have for example made their Global MD at Dow Jones also specifically responsible as Chief Customer Officer. Other companies like House of Fraser and also Tesco have responded to the new customer challenge by promoting their Heads of Digital, first to a Head of Multi-Channel role and then to the role of Chief Customer Officer with a remit to especially engage with customers in the new multi-channel world. Still others have asked their CMOs to take this formal customer responsibility, so companies like Salesforce.com, DHL and eBay have adopted that approach.

Each company is finding its own solution and fitting that person into the organisation at a level that suits their culture, where they are on the customer experience journey and how critical they see this step in comparison to their other priorities.

One of the questions many are asking is can an organisation have a CMO and a CCO at the same time? Surely both would claim responsibility for "owning the customer"? After all, is it not the CMO's job to develop communications and plans that do engage effectively with customers, that do manage the company through this multi-channel landscape, that do embrace the digital world?

At present where such roles do co-exist effectively it's where the CCO role has been clearly defined. To make that collaboration work, the CCO needs to be someone who will focus on the customer *process* through the company, who will work with IT to join-up systems so that a more complete and integrated view of the customer will emerge and so the CCO is therefore the person who builds the platform and capability that can make the campaigns and initiatives of the CMO more effective in the market place.

So it can work! but it does need a clear demarcation of responsibilities.

Is there enough of a talent pool to find these people? The answer is a definitive yes. Though some companies have stumbled as they have tried to respond to the customer "digital challenge", yet many are succeeding. As indeed the NPS scores show, there are a number who are successfully embracing these new opportunities.

The key qualifications for anyone taking a CCO role will be (i) their digital know-how and expertise, (ii) their awareness and familiarity with new technology tools and innovations and (iii) most critically, having a clear strategic view of the changing multi-channel landscape and its impact on customers.

Some of this talent pool will come from the Marketing community where they have demonstrated success in driving improvements in customer engagement and effectiveness. Others may come from a customer services / customer experience /self-serve background where they have developed skills in understanding customer need. It's possible that others may simply be smart, experienced execs who want to make a difference and have worked on the front line building businesses in the market place.

What's clear is that whatever choices a company makes, the ever-changing digital and technology challenge will not go away, that the pace of change will continue for some time and that customers will grow ever more demanding in what they expect and the sort of relationship they demand if they are to give a brand or organisation their loyalty and continuing custom.

Chapter 5

Digital HR and the "War for Talent"

We are entering a new era of what's being called: "Digital HR". Technology of course has been the major driver of change and innovation especially over the past 15 years. 86% of CEOs say that technology advances will be the key challenge in their business over the next 5 yrs (PWC survey). Every day brings new examples of how companies are looking to engage differently with their customers through new web sites, e-commerce, new mobile and social media initiatives, and using new data and front end software tools to make customer purchasing and interaction more engaging and efficient.

But now companies are beginning to turn their attention ever more closely to the internal organisation and "ways of working". Challenging how new digital technology can improve the company, make it easier for people to do their job, streamline processes and interactions, speed up what gets done and how to do it, automate to reduce error, time and costs, enhance the work environment, share and collaborate, improve job satisfaction, impact and effectiveness.

As many companies start to put the spotlight on this agenda, so HR is for sure a part of this discussion and in fact might well be seen as a leader of this technical opportunity. Many HR teams have already been "technology innovators and advocates". They have spent the past 5 /10 yrs looking for example at software as a service (SaaS) solutions, (now more "fashionably" described as Cloud-based services). The primary focus of this activity has been on cost. And that's led HR teams to outsource a range of service to SaaS providers to cut fixed costs and make the base more variable. Such has been the scale of this HR SaaS activity that this is probably one of the most competitively provided of all cloud /SaaS service areas. Indeed, the HR press has been full of headlines such as: "Aviva reduces HR costs by 30%", "Telefonica saves 40% with new Cloud platform", "Shell plans to save £Ms with new HR tools"…

But of course neither technology nor business life-cycles stay the same. With the economic outlook generally more positive, the focus and emphasis is beginning to shift. Research is showing it's less about cost reduction and more about invest to grow. And for HR teams that's creating a new imperative. It's now all about talent. If the company is to take advantage of new economic opportunities, then it's all about making sure the talent is available to drive / support that growth potential. So now research is showing that the key HR issue is: how retain what we have and how capture the best to fuel growth plans and expectations?

A recent Mercer study showed that while unemployment levels across many countries still remain high, nevertheless some 90% of HR execs said the key issue for them was talent and talent shortages: "there's a major war for good talent developing as companies now shift from containment to growth". CHROs are now putting this challenge at the top of their agenda. "we need to hang on to the people we have and we also need to find new and innovative ways to win the talent war…right now it's really difficult to get good people"

In response, some leading organisations are now looking at how digital technology innovation can help in this "war for talent". There is a move to adopt a "Digital First" strategy and in this context HR is and needs to be at the forefront.

The opportunity is: "how take advantage of new technology tools and digital solutions to improve both how we retain but also how we attract". Companies like FedEx, eBay, Cisco, HP, Procter & Gamble and Unilever have been among a number leading the charge. In fact 74% of execs in a recent PWC HR survey said they expect Digital to change the way HR operates around both existing and new talent. Most importantly, 65% said they had been encouraged by a shift in strategy and priorities to move from cost reduction in this area to investment. But only 24% said they felt their existing ways of working to support this new agenda were satisfactory. This new focus has led to new buzz phrases like "SHCM" (strategic human capital management) and "MTD" (make talent digital), but whatever the headline acronyms, it's becoming clear where the next 3 year 2018 focus will be.

What's emerging is a whole range of digital technology-led opportunities for HR teams. 7 ideas /initiatives /new tech best practices can be identified:

1. *Social Media*
2. *Video*
3. *Mobile*
4. *Gamification*
5. *Predictive Analytics*
6. *Self-serve*
7. *Dedicated HR IT*

1. Social Media

Here's a case study example from MasterCard.

In recent times, HR had been working closely with Marketing to change market, customer and employee perceptions of the company. But their research had shown that while there was plenty of external customer activity going on they had put much less emphasis on their own employees. The research showed there were gaps and weaknesses in their employee communications and there was now an opportunity to make their staff feel much more positive about the company. Achieving that would potentially not only be helping plans to retain people but would also be empowering their workforce to be external advocates for the whole organisation.

To address this, MasterCard started to look at social media. Externally that had already proven very successful with Twitter, blogs, content-driven marketing and a real time "newsroom". Their efforts had worked externally attracting millions of people globally. Now, given that success, MasterCard asked: how use social media tools to better engage internally too. How better communicate with our workforce, enable and encourage them to share, review and discuss and hopefully become a legion of new brand advocates who can turn their enthusiasm externally towards customers as well as internally among peers and colleagues.

"This year, "employee social media" is critical for us…we want to let our employees know it's ok to tweet and comment and share, it's not only ok, it's something we want to encourage"

The first thing that MasterCard needed to do was to change its internal rules about social media. To begin with there were so many constraints that people felt intimidated. So it was reduced down to a simple motto: *common sense*! Social platforms were established on Twitter, Facebook, Instagram, Pinterest, YouTube and Linkedin for employees. Introductory seminars were held where it was explained how to use and access these networks. Word got round and niche groups starting to form setting up their own social networks. For example, new employees could join a group to post comments and initial impressions and they were encouraged to be honest but did not need to state their name, they could be anonymous if they chose to.

"Key to success here has been the support of senior management to encourage people to open up, talk about issues but also themselves engage externally in the market…it's started to make a real positive impact on the way people feel about the company, the brand and MasterCard as a place to work".

MasterCard is one of many looking at this opportunity The key is to do it wholeheartedly. Often a good benchmark is whether the leadership of the company get involved. Lists for example are now beginning to appear of *top 50 CIOs who tweet*!

The PR company, Weber Shandwick, recently published a report titled: "the rise of employee activism". It showed that in most companies nearly half of all employees are active in social media and 53% expected their organisation to enable the same social dialogue and sharing internally too. The report also showed that when companies do enable their employees in this way, then they will typically also post positive external messages about the company as a place to work and about its products and services. "It's as though they feel empowered, but at the same time a sense of pride and ownership takes over that seems to encourage positive sentiment". 72% of employees in the survey said they felt encouraged to talk positively.

Weber Shandwick found that c. 30% of companies have now embraced interactive social media as a replacement for the somewhat old-fashioned / traditional "notice-board" Intranet. Of course there can be negative sentiments expressed too and while these seem to be in a minority they can be treated nevertheless as constructive and can highlight areas or issues that need intervention and attention. That social media "chatter" does need to be monitored and in extreme cases if there is abuse for example then there needs to mechanisms and resources in place for instant and remedial action. Many companies also now publish their own, though sometimes too fulsome, social media guidelines for staff and they are something new employees may be asked to sign up to when they join.

Of course Social Media has also now become a key recruitment tool. In a recent CareerBuilder /Harris report, more than 70% of companies said they now actively use social media forums to recruit. This may eg simply be about posting a job on Linkedin or CraigsList or Gumtree. It can also be about actively searching Linkedin and Facebook profiles for potential candidates or joining specialist forums which can cover just about every aspect of business from Hadoop Java engineers to dedicated CRM specialists.

This type of outbound "social media marketing" is widespread. But in the same CareerBuilder/Harris report, only 37% of companies said they used these same social media tools to screen and check on possible candidates. And only 17% said they actively check on key staff to see what they're up to on social media and look for signs and signals that they might be looking to leave and interviewing elsewhere. "a classic tell-tale sign is when an individual links up and connects with someone in a recruitment firm!"

The CareerBuilder report concludes that while lots of HR teams are using social media around talent management, most all expected their use of social media to grow substantially in the next 3 years. This was expected to include dedicated resources to actively monitor employee social media activity. But also to act as "social media talent managers"!

2. Video

Video is now being seen as a better way to communicate internally. It's more personal, more engaging and research by Accenture shows that "90% of people preferred it to more traditional forms of newsletter, round-company emails and notices posted on walls or intranets".

Video can be used widely. It need not be confined to an annual message from the CEO. In some companies like Coca Cola, Oracle, Apple and in Accenture itself, video messages are being used by Heads of a department to reach out frequently to staff all over the world with communication updates. At Wal-Mart this is being allied with regular webcasts where employees can sign in and there is Q+A to find out more or raise issues that need to be addressed. It provides the opportunity for instant updates and communication and starts to bring remote offices and workers into the company network.

What is one of the key messages that HR staff have been hearing from disgruntled employees over the years? It often comes down to: I'm not listened to, I have no voice, I might have some great ideas but there's no way to get them heard. Now video can change that. Individual teams and departments can quickly easily and at no cost make their own videos eg showcasing an idea and opportunity and can send it to a department head. It can be much more effective and impactful than being just another email.

At Google, this type of employee-led initiative and innovation is very much encouraged. It's been enshrined as one of the core reasons for the company's success. It's regarded as instrumental in keeping employees motivated as they grow. "We want everyone to feel they've got the next big idea, as we've grown we know we have to encourage discussion, exchange and reinterpretation of ideas, some of our best ideas have come about when a group of Googlers have started to talk about something that excites them, we have to enable people to realise dreams, to turn the impossible into reality, just as we believe in open technology so we believe in open access, we acquired YouTube because we believe in the power of video, so too we want employees to turn their ideas not just into words and business cases but also to bring them alive in pictures and video demonstration…"

3. Mobile

Marissa Mayer, as CEO of Yahoo!, infamously issued a mandate to all employees to "cease and desist" working from home and to come into the corporate office every day. While many saw the potential advantages of getting people together face-to-face each day, nevertheless many have argued such a mandate totally ignores best ways of working. Today's technology of course does enable remote working, whether from desktop or mobile. And indeed home working is in fact encouraged by many corporations as way of enabling a better work: life balance, making it easy for parents with families to juggle commitments but perhaps most critically the developments in mobile technology now make it very easy to engage anywhere anyhow anytime. Almost to the point where employees can be contacted 24/7/365 and that can make for too much intrusion into an individual's life… but that's another story.

For the purposes of this review, research from DynamicSignal shows that more than 50% of companies now supply senior execs with tablets to allow for remote access and collaboration. Companies like Adobe, Microsoft, Salesforce. com and Facebook now combine that with specific employee apps. These can range from dedicated apps around an upcoming Sales conference where employees can access conference info, agenda and materials all the way to motivation and e-learning tools which capture certain ideas and new initiatives like "e- Cards" which allow users to create e-card messages with graphics that can be sent easily to anyone within an organization.

The use of mobile apps for employee engagement has "risen 115%" according to research from Appirio with "more than 37% of mobile users now using mobile HR applications". This can be used for personal info eg to access their pay information, review employment contracts and conditions. This use of HR apps is especially strong nowadays where the majority of the workforce are not in a main office eg in Sales-led companies, construction, utilities etc. Companies are finding that apps are good for giving employee access to chunks of info and data but also for "pushing out information". Even to the point where the information can be sensitive to time zones and location and select what information to push out when. At PayPal for example, HR will set up a mobile app to gain specific employee feedback on a key issue asking eg the employee to vote yes or no or indicate their agreement to some idea. The feedback can be kept anonymous but it can quickly allow the company to guage employee sentiment.

Mobile is clearly an integral part of our lives and it's natural for companies to want to increasingly find ways to communicate with employees via their mobile devices. At one level it can be simple information giving, txt alerts, notices of upcoming events and at another it can become the prime means of messaging and communication. Ally that with Video and there begins a powerful combination for engaging employees in this technology-led era.

4. Gamification

This is about using play in an interactive web-based environment to motivate employees. Over the past decade, tech savvy companies have begun exploring and adapting the principles of engagement found in Gaming to better communicate with staff, make their work more fun and through that drive better performance and results.

A good example is one used by PWC in one of their recent surveys of this area. They use the analogy of the popular game Angry Birds, one of the most globally down-loaded apps. In that game the objective is to destroy as many of the target animals as possible and as you do so you win points and "get rewarded". So companies like Ford have extrapolated that principle into new ways of employee working. Simplistically for example in their Tele Sales team, the more success they have quite naturally the more reward they get. But rather than wait till end of day or end of period targets, how about more instant feedback and recognition? Just made a successful call, then up on screen is eg flash a green star, make your tenth call of the day and enter the day's lottery to win a cash prize…

Making business more "game-like" has become a big industry as technology has enabled more innovation in this area. Research firm IDC carried out an extensive study concluding: "absolutely no doubt that these techniques pay back with reports of up to 10 fold increase in employee productivity and connection with the company. Examples range from retailer Target introducing gaming into the check-out process: "fastest check-out wins", to OmniCare, the pharmacy software company, using it for Telesales, to companies like Pearson and Ford also using it in their e-Learning portal to both encourage employees to participate but also to stimulate the learning process.

It sounds obvious and simplistic and where ill-conceived it can be regarded cynically, but if carefully thought through, sensibly linked to the company's business objectives, made genuine fun and interesting it has been shown to work. "If you go into this and think I have to do this because I'm told to then it likely just won't work, but if you go into it identifying a specific task or behaviour issue which could realistically be addressed in this way, then that's how to start making Gamification work". And like many technology-led opportunities, if "mashed up" with eg video, mobile access and social media so rewarded employees can share their "badges and rewards" then all the more impactful this can become.

5. Predictive Analytics

A Deloitte study shows that today that only c. 14% of companies use "predictive analytics". This is about being able to use data to better understand the type of personality profile or background that will succeed in the company or can predict eg whether an employee will leave or stay.

In this age of big data and the range of software tools and skills available to collect, manage, search and interrogate large amounts of complex data in real time, it's becoming an area of growing interest to HR leaders. It is an investment and some do argue it's an expensive alternative to what good HR management should already be about today. But as the workforce grows, perhaps becoming more international and remote, so it's harder for the HR team to get to know people, to understand each person's individual state of mind, motivations and ambitions. So can big data analysis step in and provide some of that insight and guidance?

The Deloitte study among other things tried to demonstrate the RoI and the business case for potential investment in this area. They found that companies with stronger financial performance were typically also the ones who were using some form of predictive analytics in their HR team. These companies were working to better understand individual motivation and behaviour, pick out winning personality profiles, better develop succession planning effectiveness and identify teams and departments with the most forward potential.

An example comes from AllState Insurance. They wanted to better understand why sales performance varied very dramatically among its Sales team. They developed a model looking at performance and comparing it with a number of factors. These included the personality type identified in the assessment tests when they had joined the company, type of education, levels of school qualification, years of experience, knowledge of the company and its products and other factors. The company had thought that its best Sales people were typically people who had been educated at the top schools. The analysis showed this was not the case at all. The highest performers were in fact rarely from the top schools and usually had not been those who'd achieved the highest grades in exams. In fact the personality assessment profiles which had been outsourced and whose results had hardly been looked at were in fact the best predictors by far as to how well the employee would do in this area. It was not about demographics or years of experience or even surprisingly how well the individual salesperson understood the product range. It was all about interpersonal skills, whether introspective or extravert but how well they were able to *listen*.

6. Self-Serve

Today's web-based multi-device mobile world creates expectations of being able to do what you want and when you want to do it. While that's a key factor and driver of consumer behaviour, that set of expectations does not stop with a purchase from Amazon. It carries forward into everything people do and employee interactions with their employer are no exception. Employees want to be able to check eg on monthly salary, has it been paid, has the car allowance been included, has the promotion been finalized, what's on my 401k or my pension plan, when is the next performance review and so on. And they want to be able to do that eg on a Sunday morning at home while catching-up on private emails and paying the bills.

At first, companies looked at "self-serve" as a cost-saving exercise, eg how save headcount in payroll if we could stop all those simple query calls during the week where employees were just ringing up or stopping by to check some basic details. Some initials steps to streamline all that saw ever-lengthening lists of FAQs on the company intranet that no one looked at anyway. But companies now appreciate that while yes, encouraging self-serve can reduce costs, it has a much more powerful empowering effect. It simply puts the employee more in control, it gives them the convenience factor and helps them do their job and better understand their situation. And of course there are mobile apps enabling this too!

Universities and colleges have been among early adopters. St Helen's College in Liverpool provides a typical example. It has had an employee self-service system in place for some time. Rather than suffering the typical problem of managers and staff not being engaged to use it, its head of HR,

John Hays, says he's had to pro-actively educate and inform staff. But he found that the more he explained, then the more staff wanted to use the system!. The college's self-service system includes functions such as payroll, being able to make address and personal information amendments, booking annual leave, inputting attendance records, and online qualifications and training updates. Hays and his team carried out a staff survey recently where 90% of staff said they would welcome more online self-service.

Most self-serve initiative have been around basic payroll data. But for example, there's growing interest and use of what's described as "Manager self-serve". According to the latest PWC HR survey, 68% of companies enable their managers to complete certain selected tasks remotely and online.

At a basic level this can allow expense review and sign-off automatically connecting with payroll to add that sum to the next monthly pay. Other routine examples can be eg agreements to holiday requests or acknowledgement of medical certificates for absence from work.

Where the market is moving is in what David Woodward, CIO at Ceridian, describes as "value added" self-service systems, incorporating online appraisals, flexible benefits platforms, CV checks, interview panels, online recruitment, salary amendments and knowledge sharing. In some companies there are also examples of manager self-serve for staff promotions, reporting line changes, changes of team structure. The view is that it is possible to do this in a number of areas depending on the seniority of the manager and their experience.

As an example, one US company, Verizon, describes how it used to use Excel spreadsheets to handle compensation planning and to determine whether they had the budget to hire new personnel. Invariably, they had to contact human resources to check their own data or visit payroll to request a bump in someone's pay. Simple things seemed to take longer than necessary.

Many of those common managerial tasks became easier, when the company installed a new manager self-serve platform (there are many available from the likes of SAP and Oracle/PeopleSoft and others). The web-based software has a "manager self-service" (MSS) module that allows managers to see different screens to determine budgeting, bonus and merit pay, auditing, maximum and minimum compensation ratios, and vacation requests. Managers access the information from the company's intranet or remotely through a secure Web site.

Managers have embraced the software. "We've had a really good response, especially in the area of budgeting…managers like it quite a bit and tell us it saves them a great deal of time."

7. HR IT

With all these sort of opportunities available, there is increasing need for technology resource and investment in HR. In the recent past, HR has not usually been seen as an area for IT investment. As new IT opportunities have become available, it's more routinely been about how partner with external third party software vendors to take advantage of the technology through a SaaS type relationship. Let others worry about the software while we get on and worry about our people! And that philosophy still has many advocates and is certainly a valid and vital strategy. But with this shift in global markets, with the emphasis now more about growth than reduction, with the "war for talent" becoming perhaps the key HR issue for the next few years, and with the advent of technology that can enable and empower in the way this review has described, then perhaps now is the time to reappraise the role of IT in HR, what levels of IT enablement would be appropriate in this new business cycle and technology age and what sort of investment in fact does HR need in order to compete effectively in the talent wars while also making existing employees feel engaged, listened to and positive about the company they work for.

With that backcloth, companies are now asking these sort of questions:

- how many HR technology support resources should we have?
- how should HR technology be organised?
- should HR IT be a dedicated team?
- should that team be part of HR rather than part of IT?
- what HR tech tools are out there that we should be considering?
- should be we adopting self-serve for example or social media more vigorously and if so again what IT resources and investment do we need and what sort of payback can we expect?

The PWC survey, referred to previously, found that many HR teams did have their own IT resource which sat as part of the HR team and reported into the CHRO. But crucially, some 45% of companies said they had no formal HR IT strategy or roadmap. This was often due to some uncertainty at senior level on just how proactive HR should be in using technology. There was for example still doubt about the value of social media, mobile was seen as a nice to have rather than a necessity and there was feeling that HR's job anyway was to retain and hire the best people so why spend on technology to achieve that, better to spend on the people themselves.

What's clear is that this new age and cycle is challenging traditional ways of operating and thinking. It is opening up new ways to do business and new ways to engage with talent. But while perhaps some larger companies may be slower to adopt and adapt, for sure smaller or more agile companies will be taking advantage of technology to better connect with their people and those they want to hire. And this will inevitably set benchmarks in the market, will create the buzz and interest of things innovative and new and create expectations among other employee groups of what they could, even should expect,

Perhaps the ideas being discussed here will be everywhere in a few years' time but while laggard companies try to catch-up, the more pioneering will be able to grab advantage in this renewed war for talent.

Chapter 6

What is the HR Impact of Digital on Future Talent Needs and Hiring?

To what extent is digital changing the type of candidate that organisations are looking for? Has the arrival of this digital technology and multi-channel world changed the underlying characteristics and attributes of a successful modern day hire? Have we reached a sea-change in the type of skills, attitude and outlook that it takes to succeed?

Certainly right now there is a wide-spread view that it is hard to find good "digital" people. In a recent survey by e-Consultancy, 68% of HR professionals said they had difficulty recruiting staff who were sufficiently knowledgeable about digital technology and communications. 73% commented that digital was making a significant impact on preferred candidate profiles and 43% commented on the challenge of keeping up to date with the new digital trends and tools. What's more HR teams are having themselves to become increasingly "digitally savvy". 74% said they had had to become more skilled in using online search tools to find out about a candidate's reputation and 46% said they had rejected a candidate based on what they had discovered about a person online with Facebook, YouTube and blogs being cited as key influences.

So "Digital" is making a substantial impact in the way companies generally do organise and go to market. A recent study by BCG (Boston Consulting Group) together with Google showed that the "digital economy" is already making a substantial contribution to US and UK GDP, eg worth more than 7% of UK GDP at more than £100bn. That makes it larger than the construction, utilities and transportation sectors! And it is fast growing, expected to double over the next 5 years. At that level it will be larger than the Financial Services sector!

"Digital" is now a widely used term and it has become a catch-all umbrella for a whole range of different skills and requirements. For example within "digital marketing" there are a large number of specialist skills. These include: Search engine marketing, search engine optimisation, affiliate marketing, web analytics, campaign analysis, creative marketing, brand strategy development, customer retention, eCRM, email marketing, and now add on mobile commerce, social media and interactive TV. All these areas are unique and distinctive skill sets. They all require a candidate with specific know-how and skills. But if a business team asks for a "digital marketeer", there is often the assumption that someone with knowledge of the online world can turn their hand to any and all of these very different things. And yet what can make a difference is a candidate who really is for example, steeped and immersed in mobile, who really does have the case studies and the war stories and the lessons learnt so that they know intuitively what will drive successful mobile comms, content and commerce.

The same can be said for the technology area. In a recent survey by IBM of 2000 IT professionals, 91% said that digital technology tools would dominate by 2020 and would form the primary IT delivery model. They mentioned a wide range of skill set requirements from IT visioning and enterprise architecture, through to SOA (service-oriented architecture) and SaaS (software as a service) and Cloud computing. The IT community are also placing a much higher emphasis on Programme Management and delivery recognising that the migration to a new digital technology environment will likely need transformational change across geography and business units and will need expert tech and commercial change and delivery skills. There are also core and specialist skill requirements around IT infrastructure, data centres, data protection and security, MIS (management information services), social networks, mobile, voice recognition, content management, "green IT" and the multitude of different software programming skills from Dot Net to Java to Open Source experience to HTML5 and so on…

It's a challenging environment, it's new and there are no real proven solutions. Businesses are forced to learn and experiment as they go and make a bet, however reasoned, on what are the core skills and needs to help drive the future success and growth of the organisation. And that is often why job specs for "digital" jobs are difficult to write. Unlike for example a search for a new financial controller where there are many years of understanding and experience as to the sort of qualifications and experience required. Digital expertise is harder to define and describe. What are the right qualifications, what sort of university degree is most relevant, how evaluate years of hands-on experience, how valuable is someone who is steeped in IT generally versus a new grad who has grown up using and learning the new digital tools and environment? If there's a need for a marketer then how transferable are for example search engine marketing skills into a more general online marketing remit? If looking for a new architect how familiar and expert do they need to be in cloud computing, if according to IBM, that will be the specific area that will dominate IT development for the rest of this decade?

In summary there are probably 5 key things that can be identified from all the research and experience that distinguish a candidate who is best-suited for the digital world. The focus here is less on the specific skills eg in Search engine marketing specialisation or in SOA, but more around the qualitative attributes that mark out an individual. What is the "right stuff" that HR teams and business owners should be looking for? It's all changing so fast and hard to know what will be required in the business in 12 months time, let alone 3 years out. But can we put together a simple and sustainable check-list of core attributes and characteristics?

The 5 keys are:

1. *A restless spirit*
2. *Comfort and confident with technology (but not necessarily a "techie")*
3. *Communication and interpersonal skills*
4. *Self-sufficiency*
5. *An appreciation that it's a multi-channel world*

A restless spirit: this is someone who enjoys and relishes change! It's the individual who is happy that there is no complete job spec, who is comfortable that there is no clearly defined box for the role, it's that person who recognises that we are going through a revolution in communications and in technology and who wants to be part of that, contributing to it, challenging traditions and accepted methodologies and processes, a force for change who is unhappy if things are status quo or if things take too long to happen, an inquisitive mind who wants to know about the latest technologies and tools and is passionate about them.

Comfort and confident with technology: this is a vital prerequisite. They need not necessarily have a deep tech background if they are for example up for a marketing role, but they must have an appreciation of it, a desire to understand it and ability to talk about it. They need to know what is "cloud computing", why it's being so widely discussed and be able to see the potential commercial applications. They need to appreciate that doing something in mobile for example is not just about "creating an app for the iPhone" but that there are scores of other handsets which need to be separately managed and that configuration of the online site may require significant technical resource. They need to be a point of contact that can translate tech advances into commercial feasibility

Communication and Interpersonal skills: a recent survey by the US Center for Public Education highlighted this area as the key requirement. "The 21st Century is bringing a requirement for new skills and tools in the workspace. Strong interpersonal skills for collaboration and communication will be a "must-have" competency. It's the power to interact effectively, to communicate both face-to-face, in large and small meetings, both verbally and with data, to relate well to others and to cooperate with them, to negotiate and manage potential conflicts of priority between departments and to lead through persuasion. In times of change and especially where organisations are having to adopt new technologies and new ways of working, this is going to be a core skill".

Self sufficiency: organisations are already moving toward remote working environments. The concept of everyone travelling to an office to do a day's work and do that every day of the week is a not a 21st century way of working. Unilever for example have adopted a workplace strategy which looks at three categories of employee. They call it "resident, mobile and offsite". Residents are still those who come to work and have their own desk and workspace. That might be eg the office manager, security staff as well as others who prefer that style. The Mobile worker has typically been the salesperson out and about with customers but returning to base and hot-desking there, so having access but no "permanent home". And then the Remote worker, who may never visit the office, may be established at home or be a connected contractor or consultant or supplier who needs and gets access to fellow employees, office news and information, email etc but always from a remote station.

Unilever are also studying how the next 5 years will further change that categorisation. One thing they are certain about: there will still be a need for an office, but there will be a substantial shift from resident to mobile and offsite. This has far-reaching impact on people. Are they the sort that can cope with this change in work pattern? Are they self-sufficient in that they could be set up to eg work from home? Are they reliable in that they may have limited physical contact with colleagues and it will be harder to monitor their performance?

Appreciation it's a multi-channel world: while this has all been about digital, it is just as important for good candidates to appreciate that there is a much that is not digital. 20% of the UK population are not online, e-commerce accounts for some 15% to 20% plus of total retail and while many will research online still the majority will shop and buy in-store. TV advertising still accounts for some 40% of all advertising spend and is still the key way for any organisation wishing to build a mass wide-reaching consumer brand. 56% of consumers have smart phones with Net access but that still means a large number that do not and most people today will shop and research and interact in a multi-channel and cross platform way. So it's critical that good marketers and technology people do appreciate this, do understand that you can't just "switch off analogue" overnight, that the spread of online and digital technology will still be unfolding for the rest of this decade and that any business solution will need to accommodate customers wherever they are and through whatever channel they choose to interact.

★★★★★

It's always been a challenge of course to find the best candidates for the organisation. There will always be competition for the very best people and a premium on their time and services. But as we look at the next few years it is clear that digital is placing an added layer of complexity. There are many people who will claim to be "digital experts" and cite years of experience, but the facts are that this whole world has emerged so very recently that there just are not that many experts around. Social Media and Mobile for example only really got going at the start of this decade. So claims of "years of expertise" in those areas need to be carefully examined. Equally there has been talk about SaaS and Cloud but not many organisations and people have any genuine deep and immersed expertise and insight. This shortage then of really experienced talent puts a bigger emphasis on the 5 keys discussed here: to find those individuals with the spirit, the confidence, the interpersonal skills, the self-sufficiency and the strategic multi-channel awareness that they can operate effectively in this digital world and make the outstanding impact that they've been hired for.

Chapter 7

5 Keys to Finding the Best Digital Talent

Digital has now of course become part of every successful organisation's DNA. It has developed rapidly and offers new ways of working, quicker and more cost-effective solutions as well as providing new routes to customers and markets. It's become an engine of change as well as revenue growth and vanguard companies are experiencing substantial upsides in business.

At the same time, this catalyst for change is still a relatively new phenomenon and it means that the talent pool that has real depth of experience and expertise and know-how is relatively limited. Some companies are now saying that it is becoming very hard for them to find good "digital" talent; that they are struggling to support and develop the growth opportunities because they cannot get the right people into their teams.

But the most successful companies do not seem to find this same problem. Those who get digital, who fully embrace it from the CEO and HR to the most junior assistant, those for whom it has become their way of working and the source of growth as well as saving cost, those where there is real commitment, investment and priority behind their digital transformation programs, those are the companies that have also learned how to build a really simple but very effective digital talent-finding and recruiting model. This note looks at those best practices.

One immediate observation is that these "best practices" are far from being rocket science. In many ways they are nothing new, they are no more than what good talent finding processes should anyway be all about. But in these days when the "digital talent pool" is still growing and when there is very high demand for the best people, then these "better processes" and practices become all the more compelling.

1. The Senior management team buys into the essence of Digital as their key driver.

How many times do candidates ask this…does the management team at senior level really get this, are they paying lip service to digital technology, to Cloud and web and e-commerce and mobile, or is this centre stage of their investment strategy? Good candidates say they repeatedly come across organisations who say they want to change, to embrace these new opportunities, but who in practice are doing very little that's different.

And candidates have wised up to this. It's one of their first questions. How important is this to the Board, how critical is this to the company's agenda, what levels of budget and support will be available? How often do candidates go to an interview and ask these leading questions, only to be disappointed and frustrated by the answer. They discover that in fact they will be in effect a "lone wolf", relegated to being a "voice of influence" (sometimes euphemistically described as a "champion of change"), that there will be no team to support them, that "this year there is very little budget, but next year…"

The best candidates will not be fooled. They will have been through these foundation experiences, they will have seen the pitfalls and frustrations. They will be looking for a place where they *can* make an impact and effect change.

Needless to say those organisations who want to do something but who don't back up the words with substantive commitments will not attract and get the best people.

2. Acknowledging that this need for digital-led change is now urgent and that all is not perfect!

Many companies are relatively weak in their digital know-how today, their IT legacy systems are poor and unsuited to new ways of working, their online environment is not optimised for the user experience and concepts of fundamental IT innovation are discussed but rarely pursued.

Yet in candidate interviews, it's as though there's a big cover-up. Instead of acknowledging the weaknesses or better put, "the opportunities for change", the interview is more about joining the team, fitting-in with existing work patterns, joining the culture, about gentle evolution when sometime more progressive and radical action is required.

But, the best digital talent is usually passionate about what can be done, big believers in what new technology solutions can achieve and wants to find an environment where they can practice what is preached. And be able to do so with immediate effect. As soon as they sense an organisation is slow or reluctant then once again they will themselves be very hesitant about joining such a culture.

3. A fast recruitment process

Good candidates respond positively and enthusiastically when the company also operates in that same way. From brief to first contact to final interview the process should take just a few weeks. It should not take months. And unfortunately months is the timeframe that many, often apparently very sophisticated large companies, will operate in. How many times does a business /function leader give out a brief, only for it then to stall while others sign-off, and then the key interviewer is busy or travelling or away, and then several weeks go by after the first interview before the second interview is set-up and then similar long gaps, and while for the candidate this process is potentially very much the centre of their whole world as they contemplate what for them is a big career move, this same sense of priority, of importance, of care and concern is often just not mirrored by the interviewing company.

Disillusion can quickly set in as the candidates starts to question: is this role really important to the company, are they committed to this new venture /initiative, they might be giving me good feedback but do they really want to make this hire, why do I have to wait weeks to hear if there is going to be a next step.

These delays should be the exception, but in practice they are common. Suffice to say that in this "war for good digital talent" those who interview quickly and positively get the best people.

4. Some salary/ comp. flexibility

Because "digital" is new, because the talent pool is limited, because things are changing fast, then to maximise recruitment success, the learning is the need for at least some salary /comp. package flexibility.

Of course it's understood by candidates that the company will have salary bands at different levels in the company, that the compensation needs to approximately match up to peers, and that the new digital exec cannot be too much out of line.

But the fact is that there is a premium on salary levels for the best talent. That the best people will be paid well, that if it comes to making an offer, then the best out of this limited talent pool might just justify a premium to the base pay, or some kind of "sign-on" signature, or some higher grant of options or some inducement that does reflect their worth in the market.

It sometimes happens that a candidate will turn down job opportunities for roles they would be brilliant for simply because at the final negotiation the salary offered was below expectations or was less than that from a more progressive rival company.

Why is it that Google, Apple, Amazon and eBay are regarded as having the best digital talent today? One reason is that they did not compromise in paying the best salary levels to attract the top talent. Their mantra is: "the best companies should attract the best people". It might have been regarded as a significant investment in their early days to pay high compensation levels but they argue that that investment has more than paid back with their continued streams of market-leading innovations.

5. Measure how effective the recruitment process is /where it can be improved

There are certain key metrics which enable an organisation to measure how effective it is at finding and recruiting the best people:

- *average time a job role is open*
- *ave. number of candidates interviewed per role*
- *ave. number of interviews a candidate has*
- *time from brief to offer*
- *% offers accepted*
- *ave. salary premium if any*
- *time from brief to candidate starting*
- *ave. length of time new hire stays with the company*
- *% who stay > 2 years*

This dashboard /scorecard, combined with other metrics key to a specific organisation, can be kept and monitored. It may just highlight where things can be improved!

★★★★★

Finally, let's acknowledge that there are many brilliant people out there but they don't all need to be a rockstars to make a superb contribution

Recent work by a combined HR team from Caterpillar, General Mills and Schlumberger showed that a key delaying factor in recruitment was being too idealistic and setting unrealistic expectations of the profile and required abilities in the job description and brief.

The research showed that briefs often set out a "wish list" of desired attributes and expertise. And it concluded that often times no candidate could realistically be expected to match that wish list! It also showed that against those search criteria the level of salary offered often just would not be enough to attract that sort of person anyway.

So companies will frequently set off down a path where it will be very hard to find the right match. Hence there is delay and frustration with the process. The recommendation from the research is, put simply, be realistic!

There are many talented people out there who will do a very good, honest and often a tremendous job, but they are not all rockstars! They don't all walk on water! And do they need to, to do this particular job really well?

> *"Hire people with potential, give them the opportunity to spread their wings, put the right compensation behind them, watch them fly"*
> – Jack Welch, previous CEO of GE

> *"It's not about the coffee, it's about the people and growing and nurturing and teaching then so they can fulfil their potential"*
> – Howard Behar, founder of Starbucks

> *"Get the team together, only then can you make something happen"*
> – Thomas Watson, former President of IBM

Chapter 8

How the Workplace will Change and the Workforce will Need to Adapt

What will be the impact of digital transformation on the 2020 workplace? Will office life still be more or less the same, will we still have an office to go to, will we all need to become tech geeks and programmers, will be still be typing on Microsoft Word or will be talking to our computer and using VRS, will we still meet and socialise with our co-workers and have office friends and networks or we simply interact remotely, how global will be our remit or will we still act and think within local country boundaries, will there still be specific function groups eg for Marketing and IT or will we all need to become multi-skilled, multi-channel experts?

For sure, the workplace will have changed and there are 7 key themes that will characterise this change:

1. Mobile: meaning same speed instant screen access from anywhere
2. Anytime: 24/7/365 communication
3. Democratisation: more people involved
4. Flatter hierarchies: less emphasis on managing downwards/upwards and more on contribution and engagement
5. The "Knowledge worker"
6. Global: no boundaries
7. Automation: a lot of what we do today will be done automatically by machines.

Let's consider each of these:

1. Mobile: At Unilever, as in most every other organisation, the culture and expectation used to be that people would come to work. They would clock-in or register or at least make their presence felt and be available. Today, Unilever's policy has shifted to accommodate three types of employee. What they call:

resident, mobile and offsite. Residents are still those who come to work and have their own desk and workspace. That might be the Office manager, security staff as well as others who prefer that style. The Mobile worker has typically been the Salesperson out and about with customers but returning to base and hot-desking there, so having access but no "permanent home". And then the remote worker, who may never visit the office, may be established at home or be a connected contractor or consultant or supplier who needs and gets access to fellow employees, office news and information, email etc but always from a remote station.

While that may be a simple but very appropriate way to think about the workplace today, Unilever also are studying how the next 10 years will change that categorisation. One thing they are certain about: there will still be a need for an office, but there will be a substantial shift from resident to mobile and offsite. This has far-reaching impact on the size and amount of office space required. It also and most especially impacts the IT and communications systems that must enable people to still work effectively in teams and make informed and pragmatic decisions while perhaps never meeting in person.

"The challenge we have is that most of our employees do like coming to work, they enjoy the learning and stimulation of working with colleagues as well as the social interaction. The advent of digital technology allows us to find new ways of working and collaborating but they will also require us to get used to a different type of "office life".

So the trend to mobile and offsite will continue to grow, it may be driven as much by pressures to continue to reduce costs as by the availability of technology and what it can easily enable. One stark message here for the commercial property industry: will we still need the same amount of office space in 2020? Surely, companies will be reviewing just how many people they really do need to house in the future. If a persuasive business and HR case can be made for encouraging mobile and offsite then it will be accompanied by the need for fewer square feet. That might impact the major business centres less than the secondary ones. Companies might still feel they "need a presence in the City" for example, but business parks in secondary and tertiary locations may well struggle to retain occupancy rates.

This physical space dilemma is no different than the one discussed facing retail organisations. As online shopping becomes more and more attractive and easy, retailers will need fewer shops. And only now after years of the "doom mongers" saying that there is a real estate time bomb waiting to go off, are retailers truly beginning to review their shop portfolio and space needs over the next 10 years. Such are the leadtimes that it can easily take up to 10 years from design to build to occupancy. If the future does require less physical office space then it may soon be time to sell stock in commercial property developers!

2. Anytime: The ubiquity of computers and mobile devices will increase expectations of immediate interaction and response. Consumers already expect 24/7/365 access to the internet, to online shopping (ever seen a web site notice saying closed for the weekend!), to call centres, to get technical support whenever needed, access to bank accounts and money transfers, the availability of advice and service when they want it and wherever they are. As that consumer demand continues to grow, all forms of customer service will need to provide round the clock support. Gone will be the days that people will accept "our office hours are open 9 to 5 Monday till Friday".

Metro Bank is just one of the new organisations to recognise this. It has been a pioneer in retail banking offering 7 day week branch opening hours 8 till 8. Will we for example see other financial institutions follow? Most have now recovered from the old '08 banking crisis but have frustratingly reverted to their old ways, shored up by recovering profits. No need or urgency to change just yet? But expect continued customer demand and pressure for convenience to continue to drive retail and banking innovation. And if these changes follow through, they may become part of a universal trend to offer a continuous "we never close" service and facility.

And all that means that the workforce will need to adapt to that pattern. It's already happened in retail where some stores open 24 hours and of course the Manufacturing sector, with its high fixed cost asset base, has long ago implemented 24/7 shift patterns and working practices to leverage that cost base and investment.

In today's world of competitiveness, the end of the "job for life" philosophy, cost and other pressures, few jobs are truly "safe" and the workforce has had to become more adaptable and flexible to keep its jobs and its wages. So accepting shift patterns, having a willingness to work "nights" while having the day off, participating in global teams and ventures which may conflict with historic social /relaxation at home with family patterns, may become more widely adopted and accepted as the normal way of doing business and holding down a job. In fact most managers today, especially if they are involved in a global company, find they have to have a huge amount of 24/7 flexibility. Time zones mean that a US company dealing with a partner organisation or with colleagues working in China has only a limited window of same day time to set up video and conference calls. The need to often just do that means that if a manager in San Francisco wanted to speak to a colleague in Shanghai on the same day then that call would have to be no later realistically than 06.00 PST, as the time in Shanghai at 16 hours ahead would be 22.00. And it's becoming increasingly common for execs who want to have a "quiet chat" with a colleague or investor or recruit away from the rush of the day job, to book conference calls during the weekend.

A Gartner report looking at the 2020 workplace makes this prediction: "many employees will have neither a company-provided physical office nor a desk and their work will increasingly happen 24 hours a day, seven days a week. This will create issues as the lines between personal, professional, social and family matters will disappear"

3. Democratisation: A recent McKinsey report on Web 2.0 found that companies who actively encourage wide-spread internal and social networking were more successful than those that did not. The report identified twelve specific web networking technology tools which could contribute to make that difference. These included: *blogs, mash-ups (applications that eg combine multiple sources of data into a single tool), microblogging, peer to peer, podcasts, prediction markets ("the wisdom of crowds"), rating, RSS (Really Simple Syndication), social networking, tagging, video sharing, and wikis.*

And encouraging this internal sharing and discussion and collaboration and keep up to date communication was found to produce benefits in a number of areas. Increased employee satisfaction was near the top of the list as employees were discovering new ways to contribute and feel part of a community with a shared purpose. And the company found benefits in reduced operating costs and an increasing number of successful innovations to the working practices resulting in increased speed of decision-making and faster time to market.

Sounds like this is the way all companies should be moving. A demonstrable and proven way to make a company work in a digital environment. Benefits to both employee and employer. Potentially easy to implement even though many companies struggle without a unified messaging and collaboration platform, disparate systems, no connected-up intranet, firewalls or policies restricting access to the world wide web or to social networks specifically. But at the end of the day they don't need much more than a web browser and a password protected environment. And there are companies who are already out there and making this Web 2.0 internal socialising work.

Dresdner Bank uses an internal knowledge-sharing "socialtext wiki" to manage meeting agendas and capture the key points and conclusions to provide an easily accessible record and archive trail of project progress open to all. Dell has an active social networking programme that reaches out to customers but also seeks to engage internally to help unify a geographically diverse global work force. And instead of waiting for the next CEO podcast, everyone is encouraged to blog, set up their own community groups whether work-related or not and to participate in discussion forums. Walt Disney, Oracle/ Sun Microsystems and even General Motors are finding these techniques valuable in both communicating their own corporate messages but also giving everyone in the company a voice and most importantly a channel to be heard.

This is the digital equivalent of the water cooler conversation. It's been heralded as one of the biggest changes in a century in the way companies organise and communicate internally. While much was made of the intranet, it did typically rely on corporate IT to establish some unnecessarily complex solution which took 2 years to build, cost millions, didn't work well, had an appalling user interface and noone used. This time around web technology makes it easy, the interface can be simple, Facebook can be the template, keep it hosted in the cloud, adopt a standard keyword search facility and let the users populate and paint the space. As a recent piece of Forrester research on the subject commented: "the product or process is owned by all the people who create it, wherever they are in the creation process, it drives a collective sense of ownership and responsibility".

4. Flatter hierarchies: today's classic hierarchical organisation structure is not fit for the 2020 work place. The new technology world and the tech socials who will drive it will require a more collaborative and cooperative way of working. "Command and Control" hierarchy will need to give way to "Autonomy and Empowerment". Looser team-based designs will need to be adopted that replace today's multi-layered approach where we often find managers managing managers!

As Charles Handy, one of the great strategists of recent times has pointed out: "there is no logic which says that the sequence of decision-making needs to be turned into a vertical ladder so that those who make the early decisions are higher up in the hierarchy than those who implement them. And as history has shown, the larger the organisation the more complex the hierarchy and the greater the bureaucracy".

"Destructured" organisation design is now being recognised as a form more suited to a fast-paced competitive environment which needs to be able to adapt quickly, make more immediate decisions and better harness the skills and expertise of the *whole* workforce. The buzz words are all about "flexibility, speed, integration and innovation". And the magic number is 50.

50 is regarded as the size of structure and team where everyone can know everyone else, where it's possible to establish critical mass in terms of the variety of skills and experience, where people can easily communicate and collaborate, where decision-making can be quick, where "office politics" can be kept to a minimum and where a true sense of collective ownership can be fostered. Structure can be kept to small teams and team leaders where there is less emphasis on managing and more on doing and contributing. This can generate a sense of empowerment and a feeling that each person is responsible. It's no longer about "I did my bit", but more about "this is mine and we've all got to get it right!"

And yes, this may sound somewhat utopian and the many who are involved today in a large corporate with all its established structures and ways of working may wonder how it is possible to migrate from the current to the new. But the forces for change will come both externally from the market place and the need to be competitive but also internally from the new generation of the workforce who will be making their own imprint on how they work and how best to organise.

HP, Xerox, General Electric are example of big companies who have nevertheless been pioneers of flatter structures. GE was the archetype of the top-down, command-and-control structured company. But they have found ways to re-design their structure so that the divisions run as smaller entrepreneurial units. One of their techniques was to introduce the term "boundaryless management". This was a direct and persistent attack on their traditional vertical structure. Siemens, before restructuring had 12 layers of management. After restructuring, it had considerably fewer. By proceeding cautiously, it managed its transition in a way that still protected the company's reputation as a good employer. Edward Jones, the US stockbroker, moved to make itself a flat company by structuring as a confederation of autonomous entrepreneurial units. They are nevertheless still bound together by a central set of shared core values and service ethics. The company today is a network of brokers, each of whom works from their own remote but connected office. Companies like Apple and Google are leaders among the new wave who have built their foundations on these same principles. It is becoming the preferred way of working for the new breed of tech companies who have the flexibility and agility to embrace digital technology in this changing landscape.

5. The Knowledge worker: The great business guru Peter Drucker has succinctly described the fundamental shift brought about by the last 10 to 15 years of technology revolution:

"The traditional factors of production – land, labour and capital have not disappeared, but they have become secondary. They can be obtained and easily obtained provided there is knowledge. Knowledge is the new means to obtain social and economic results. It is becoming the only meaningful resource"

Knowledge has become power and it is estimated that more than 1.5 trillion dollars (GigaOm) a year is being invested worldwide in developing new information and communication technologies, software and hardware to exploit knowledge as a driving source of innovation and advantage. It is also estimated that in developed countries three-quarters of the workforce can now be categorised as involved in knowledge work or service (forty years ago that would have been about one third).

The implications are far-reaching for the type of work environment and for the skills people need. Digital knowledge capture, sharing and insight become the new order. Traditional tasks become automated, software carries out the routine and commodity functions, workflow process gets managed by digital communications, paper does eventually become peripheral and people become displaced and dispersed as a more virtual world of remote information and know-how take over.

It places a whole new emphasis on "organisation design" and training and how to manage and get the best out of teams. "Knowledge workers" have become the new champions of the workforce and Computer Weekly in one article dubbed them the "new elite". Those who understand the technology, who are technically literate themselves, who know the basics of architecture and programming, who are up-to-speed with latest software and hardware in so far as it relates to their industry, who have an awareness of how the technology environment around them will evolve, whose understanding is intuitive enough that they can make the technology work for them, rather than be subjected to it…these are the sort of people who may well deserve be to be called the "elite" in this decade. Some people grow up with an innate affinity to technology and to IT generally, others will need to be trained in and learn the requisite skills. Whether a salesperson or a marketer, a finance controller or an analyst, corporate careers will need to be built on a thorough understanding of digital technology and how to leverage and harness the knowledge and insight that can be derived from it.

Knowledge work components

Knowledge work is an interaction between:

- Technology
- Information
- Humans
- Organizations

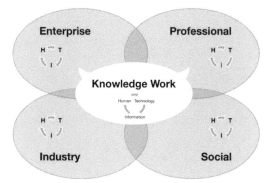

Source: PARC, Mark Bernstein

Xerox embarked on a knowledge project to capture the know-how and expertise of their 25,000 strong service technician workforce that was based all over the world. They realised there was so much knowledge and know-how that was left with the individual that there was a lot of expertise being lost and huge amount of duplication and time invested in working out answers to the same problem. Extensive documentation was, it was felt, not the answer, as their research showed that most technicians could fix most problems. Instead it was the unexpected and the unpredictable that caused delay and customer, as well as technician, frustration.

Xerox's research centre in Palo Alto, PARC, set about working on a new technology solution, it was based around the idea of establishing a social or "water-cooler" network where the shared gossip and experience could be captured and easily accessed. Through multiple field observations and design testing, PARC scientists developed a knowledge-sharing system that codified technicians' tacit know-how, lessons learned, tips and ideas.

It was recognised that to make this work, the technology environment that was created had to be "90% a social process", that its use would evolve over time, that technicians would need to be trained into both the process, how to use it and how to input to it. "Our aim has been to create an intelligent work space that users can adapt and take from it what would be helpful so it becomes a part of their natural process and interactions. We have tested it in different organisational settings and placed high emphasis on the socio-cultural factors of new technology use and adoption"

6. Global – no boundaries: A recent PWC report has been examining the increasingly global nature of the economy. Their key conclusions are no surprise. The world is "getting smaller", 25% of the global workforce is expected to be based in India and a further 20% in China, the aging population in developed countries means a third of workforce there will be over 50 with the possibility that leadership in technology and innovation shifts to a younger, more entrepreneurial Asian business community, cultural and language barriers will continue to decline as social and community networking becomes further established and entrenched, trade tariffs and other artificial barriers will become harder to maintain and senior business leaders will have to have the confidence and skills to step outside geographic and other boundaries and embrace the "global village"

The biggest challenge as already touched upon is that work can be done anywhere. This does not just mean outside the office at home, but in any country anywhere that has adequate communication connections. And the advent of Cloud computing simply reinforces this trend. In a recent review the Economist described how, just as servers, storage and desktops are becoming a "virtual cloud", so we are moving to a point where the labour element of IT will also start to become virtualised". Combine this with a universal skills vocabulary, a universal business language and lower wage costs and we quickly get to a scenario where to keep their jobs the workforce will potentially have to be especially flexible and adaptable, willing to learn but also potentially ready to locate to wherever the knowledge centres of excellence are based.

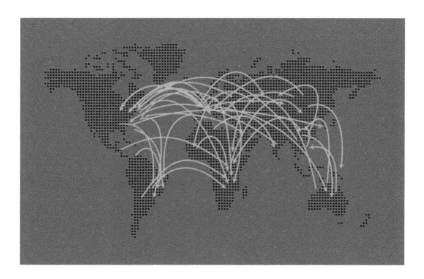

Of course the "exodus" of jobs from west to east, the brain drain, the growing power of Asian economies, the lower wage rates, the entrepreneurial spirit which is already strong in the developing economies and BRIC in particular has been well-documented and Armageddon scenarios have been variously touted and rehearsed predicting massive unemployment and declining economic prospects among western countries. But those scenarios have been around for some time and we are still yet to see any substantial impact other than slow and incremental change while in fact the major global innovators are still being born out of the west coast of the US, just as they have been for the past 30 years.

What has shifted fundamentally is the mindset required to operate effectively. It has to be global and strategies which are only local in scope are potentially missing big opportunities. That is going to be a key part of the competitive landscape through till 2020 – envisaging and identifying how to scale a new initiative quickly across the world while it is fresh and innovative and different and before it's copied and reengineered by countless others. The new entrepreneurs of the day are coming to market with this way of thinking. The world of boundaries and borders just does not exist. If we can quickly and easily participate in a virtual game with someone in China then why can't we just as easily do business together as well?

7. Automation: Is automation a job killer or a job creator? The international market for automation-related products is estimated at c. Euro300 billion according to Forbes and growth is estimated at 6 to 10% per annum. In Germany, for example, that translates into a Euro 35 billion market place. And, most importantly, it employs some 230,000 people. It has become a major contributor to Germany's electronics industry. It has become so wide-spread that it actually reinforces the attractiveness of Germany as a top industrial location encouraging new companies to set up both domestically and from overseas and all establishing new jobs. Inevitably the skill requirements for these companies require a good to high degree of technology literacy but every organisation requires people at all levels to make things happen. In fact so important is this industry as a job creator that it attracts high level political and state support.

However technology-based industries do not typically promise the same number of local jobs as asset-based production or retail businesses would have. Compare Google with McDonalds: McDonalds employs some 400,000 people worldwide, revenue per average worker of c. $60,000. Google however employs around 50,000 people at average revenue of c. $1.5m each. The question asked is: what if McDonalds were to become more like Google because of the level of production automation it was able to introduce? Would it keep the same number of employees but shift the work focus to other areas of value-add and customer service? Or would it simply reduce the number of people on its payroll?

A 2020 Gartner study considered that the worst case scenario would be characterised by substantial broad-based structural unemployment as machines do more and more of the work that was previously done by people. To avoid such a situation, the Gartner research highlighted that the need for flexibility and adaptability among the workforce would be the key. Moving to where the work is, being ready to reskill and learn new methods and applications, working to contract rather than a job for life, part-time instead of full time, working remotely and not in an office, working for small independent companies rather than big institutions as the smaller organisation takes advantage of the cloud to harness numerous remote supporting technologies and partnerships, self-improvement to continue to learn and develop…all these things will become part of the 2020 work scene. And with it our schools and universities will urgently need to adapt their courses to have an increasing vocational and pragmatic rather than academic output.

★★★★★

Let's leave the final word on the changing 2020 workplace to Philip Tidd, when partner at DEGW /Aecom, the global strategy consultancy: "What we do know is that in 2020 work will have left the building. Synchronicity and co-location are being turned on their head by new generations and new technology. People will no longer need to be in the same place at the same time every day. We will not need an office, we will connect virtually, the type of work we do will change and the way we interact and depend upon computers will experience a step change too. What we do know is that this will happen. What we don't know is how quickly it will happen or what all the consequences are"

Chapter 9

How to Structure and Organise the Digital Team
Introducing the Digital /Multi-Channel Value Chain.

Recent research from McKinsey shows a key agenda item is all around: *how should companies best organise to capture the increasingly critical digital opportunity?*

Some 63% in a recent survey said that they were unsure how to structure and fit digital skills into their existing teams. 31% felt that digital was now requiring a totally new look at skills, teams, reporting lines and ways of working. 27% also commented that "integrating new digital talent" was proving "surprisingly difficult!"

So what's causing this challenge and uncertainty? No-one doubts the importance of digital. Most every company, whether B2C or B2B, has seen how customers are demanding an increasingly online, automated, self-serve environment, how the customer expectation has rapidly developed for a seamless, integrated multi-channel experience, how getting that customer experience right can genuinely add incremental revenue and growth. So the need for people with digital skills and talent to drive this is clear. Whether in SEO or SEM, or effective e-mail marketing, or in user experience and site conversion, or in customer retention and CRM /database management, in site analytics or social media, whether via mobile or desktop…all these areas are acknowledged skills and areas of expertise which most every company nowadays recognises it needs to have.

The challenge seems to lie in the sheer size and range of new skills that a company must now embrace. Should we hire in all these different skills or can we focus on just a few, how can we budget for all this, can we see a way to get a return on this investment, how add these skills to the organisation while not upsetting the existing and still successful traditional routes to market and the people, experience and capabilities that go with that?

All the current advice on this seems to stay at the macro /30,000 feet level. It tries to answer questions like should there be a Chief Digital Officer, should digital report to the CMO or the CTO, should digital stand alone as a separate function or should it be integrated into one total group? But there's little or no advice below those big questions. They are still important but once they've been decided then how organise the next level down? How structure the junior and mid-level managers and their teams? Where do they fit in?

This note sets out a possible solution for this. It looks below the Director level, below the CMO or the CTO or the CDO! It takes a view as to how to organise the key skills at the coalface, the experts who are doing the detailed digital and multi-channel campaign, customer and business development.

To help with this we can identify a series of key principles and guiding criteria:

i. *Set up the structure with no more than 6 direct reports to the c-Level exec in charge.*
ii. *Keep it simple and manageable*
iii. *Make it measurable!*
iv. *Set things up in a multi-channel way so that that digital is integrated and not separated.*
v. *Establish the team so that together they can take one holistic and seamless view of their customer.*
vi. *Identify the key metrics and targets that can drive to a clear RoI on the persons or teams hired*
vii. *Keep it flexible: digital is evolving fast and areas like content, social media, mobile and self-serve are becoming increasingly key drivers of success. They may at some point deserve and require more prominence in the team structure.*

Recent studies from WPP's Millward Brown, from e-Consultancy and also Digital-360's own on-the-ground experience show that this desired digital and multi-channel skills set can best be categorised or structured into 6 key skill areas. We can describe those categories as forming the *"multi-channel value chain"*.

The 6 key areas are:

- **Strategy** *(that includes Brand and Product strategy and road-mapping)*
- **Brand Awareness**
- **Consideration** *(eg the content, social media, collateral that the prospective purchaser considers)*
- **Lead Generation** *(getting people onto the web site or eg into the call centre)*
- **Conversion** *(getting the sale)*
- **Retention** *(getting the customer to come back /make the next purchase, the "customer lifetime value").*

We can map this out in this way.

Figure 1:

The Digital Value Chain: the 6 core areas

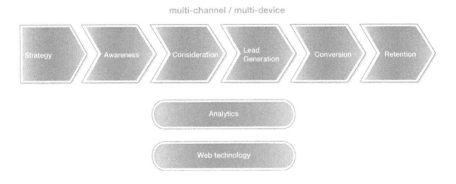

This assumes back end technology, infrastructure, project management, budgeting and finance are a shared service resource which a Commercial team can draw on and leverage.

What we are looking at here is in effect the 6 key "Heads of Department" who would report into the c-Level Exec. They may each be directors in their own right. Or they may be "heads of" depending on size and type of company, resources and budgets and ultimately the level of ambition that the total company has. It's all about getting digital /multi-channel working at its most powerful and deliver its greatest potential.

So what's in each of these 6 departments or teams and why distinguish these 6 particular categories and stages in the value chain?

We can list out (Table.2) the key areas of skill, remit, task and responsibility that each of these team heads can be expected to cover. The chart /table here is not intended to be exhaustive and it's certainly not a job profile. But it is a high level view of what can be expected and what's involved.

And this listing helps reinforce why these 6 distinct team areas have been defined and identified. It is because each area is specialist in its own right. Each does require particular and specific skills and expertise. Someone for example who is expert on UX may not also be expert at Product Strategy development. Equally, someone who is engaged in social media and content development will not necessarily be the best skilled person to eg drive database insight and CRM programmes. The skills are different. And to get the best from the team then the most efficient way to organise is to recognise that difference and structure accordingly.

Figure 2:

The Digital Value Chain: the key role details

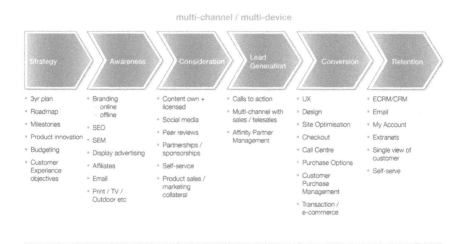

multi-channel / multi-device					
Strategy	**Awareness**	**Consideration**	**Lead Generation**	**Conversion**	**Retention**
• 3yr plan	• Branding	• Content own + licensed	• Calls to action	• UX	• ECRM/CRM
• Roadmap	• online offline	• Social media	• Multi-channel with sales / telesales	• Design	• Email
• Milestones	• SEO	• Peer reviews	• Affinity Partner Management	• Site Optimisation	• My Account
• Product innovation	• SEM	• Partnerships / sponsorships		• Checkout	• Extranets
• Budgeting	• Display advertising	• Self-serve		• Call Centre	• Single view of customer
• Customer Experience objectives	• Affiliates	• Product sales / marketing collateral		• Purchase Options	• Self-serve
	• Email			• Customer Purchase Management	
	• Print / TV / Outdoor etc			• Transaction / e-commerce	

In early digital /multi-channel times, there was not the insight, the budgets, the returns available to start building out big teams with this sort of definition and distinction. Companies hired eg a "digital manager" and asked them to kind of oversee, well everything. Do the Search, the emails, the online advertising, the customer development, the e-commerce, the mobile app development etc. It is only in very recent times, that the scale and size of the multi-channel opportunity has grown such that this level and size of team does become possible and the RoI can be seen and quantified.

There is no question that it is a virtuous circle. Set up the team correctly, make that commitment and investment, set key goals and measures of success, target a clear RoI and drive toward that.

Figure 3:

The Virtuous Circle!

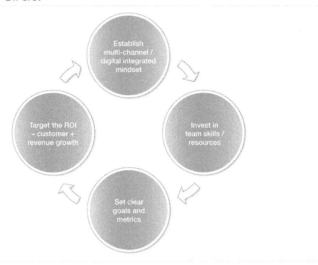

Table. 4 below now shows the metrics of success, the drivers of that RoI and customer /revenue growth. It immediately shows again how very different each role is. It demonstrates clearly that a company needs its team defined and set up carefully so that there are expert people, with the right skills, able and empowered to focus on a specific set of goals.

Setting things up along these lines makes the job of the c-Level exec in charge of all this all the more manageable and achievable. That person now has 6 key reports. Each is responsible for a core and specific part of the customer multi-channel value chain. Each is tasked with a clear set of deliverables and metrics. A KPI dashboard can be set up incorporating the key metrics from each team at each stage of the chain. Success is all about getting all 6 teams to report continuing growth in their key metrics and ratios. Each is both a cost centre as well as a profit centre. If they are contributing in the right way, then their team is delivering. They can put forward investment proposals in their area and identify their potential RoI. That might be more resource or more funds or a new product /feature/service launch. But each step is therefore measurable and all the more manageable for it.

Figure 4:

The Digital Value Chain: the key role metrics

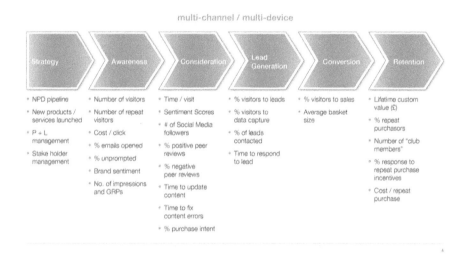

multi-channel / multi-device

Strategy	Awareness	Consideration	Lead Generation	Conversion	Retention
• NPD pipeline	• Number of visitors	• Time / visit	• % visitors to leads	• % visitors to sales	• Lifetime custom value (£)
• New products / services launched	• Number of repeat visitors	• Sentiment Scores	• % visitors to data capture	• Average basket size	• % repeat purchasors
• P + L management	• Cost / click	• # of Social Media followers	• % of leads contacted		• Number of "club members"
• Stake holder management	• % emails opened	• % positive peer reviews	• Time to respond to lead		• % response to repeat purchase incentives
	• % unprompted	• % negative peer reviews			• Cost / repeat purchase
	• Brand sentiment	• Time to update content			
	• No. of impressions and GRPs	• Time to fix content errors			
		• % purchase intent			

★★★★★

Any organisation research will always make the same observation: what is right for one company may not be right for another. Effective organisation structure depends as much as anything on the company culture, where it puts its priorities, its readiness to invest, its status on the digital /multi-channel journey, the impact that digital is having on its customer behaviour and preferences and the size of the digital prize.

In addition, investment in this area will also be driven by the c-Level team. Some teams are inherently conservative and cost conscious, they take an incremental budget /costing /next 12 months approach and will always be reluctant to add to head count unless absolutely essential. Other teams may have more flexibility because their core business is doing well or because they intuitively see the bigger 3 to 5 year picture and recognise that if they don't invest in this area now then shareholder value may start to erode significantly as they potentially struggle to compete in a digital future.

Whatever the right solution for an organisation, then it's also important to stay flexible. Digital is moving and changing as we know fast and unpredictably. No-one was able to forecast the impact of the iPhone or iPad, few today yet understand the impact of digital 3D printing, or how social media is increasingly replacing paid traditional advertising, or how mobile on-the-go connectivity is replacing the desktop and laptop. It's a changing world of course and as companies organise their teams in this area it's important to constantly review the right skills and resources are in the right places!

Chapter 10

Digital Value Chain

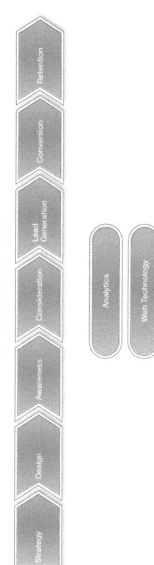

The digital value chain needs careful consideration

multi-channel / multi device

Strategy → Design → Awareness → Consideration → Lead Generation → Conversion → Retention

Analytics

Web Technology

This assumes back end technology, infrastructure, project management, budgeting and finance are a shared service resource which a Commercial team can draw on and leverage.

www.digital-360.com

The digital value chain needs careful consideration

multi-channel / multi device

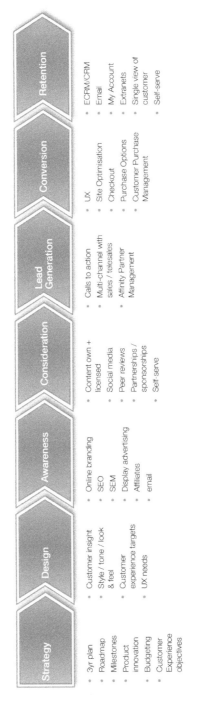

Strategy	Design	Awareness	Consideration	Lead Generation	Conversion	Retention
• 3yr plan • Roadmap • Milestones • Product innovation • Budgeting • Customer Experience objectives	• Customer insight • Style / tone / look & feel • Customer experience targets • UX needs	• Online branding • SEO • SEM • Display advertising • Affiliates • email	• Content own + licensed • Social media • Peer reviews • Partnerships / sponsorships • Self-serve	• Calls to action • Multi-channel with sales / telesales • Affinity Partner Management	• UX • Site Optimisation • Checkout • Purchase Options • Customer Purchase Management	• ECRM/CRM • Email • My Account • Extranets • Single view of customer • Self-serve

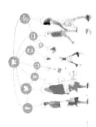

It is crucial to think and plan to organise in this way
Each area is different requiring different skills and success metrics

multi-channel / multi device

Strategy	Design	Awareness	Consideration	Lead Generation	Conversion	Retention
• NPD pipeline • New products / services launched • P + L management • Stake holder management	• Page views • Time / Visit • No of click-throughs • % increases in awareness / conversion • Sentiment scores • Awards / recognition	• Number of visitors • Number of repeat visitors • Cost/click • % emails opened • % unprompted • Brand awareness	• Time/visit • Sentiment Scores • # of Social media followers • % positive peer reviews • % negative peer reviews • Time to update content • Time to fix content errors	• % visitors to leads • % visitors to data capture • % of leads contacted • Time to respond to lead	• % visitors to sales • Average basket size	• Lifetime customer value (£) • % repeat purchasors • Number of "club members" • % response to repeat purchase incentives • Cost/repeat purchase

Chapter 11

Building a Leading E-Commerce Business: The 3 Pillars
Get 'em, convert 'em, get 'em back!

How should we organise our e-commerce team? Sales are growing, visits to the web site are up, we're recently launched mobile apps, we've got Facebook pages and Twitter feeds and we've got a reasonable-sized team, but how can we take things to the next level of sales growth and profitability? Can we define what are the key skills we should be employing, what are the right interfaces with the rest of the business, should we outsource more, or less, should we have our own technical platform, what do we need to do to be sure we've got the right structures and resources in place to make our e-commerce operation one of the best, and if we continue to invest in this area what kind of ROI should we expecting?

Most companies now have established online businesses and in today's competitive market places, many are finding that online has become the key source of growth. It is not only generating sales in its own right, and often significant levels of business, but where it is effectively integrated, it is also acting as a strong multi-channel sales tool driving footfall to stores or leads to the call centre, whether through explicit methods like "ring 'n reserve" or "live call back" or by providing a helpful, easy online experience with a clear call to action.

With all this development taking place, it is becoming ever more critical to get the online environment to really work to its best. The potential is clearly there but the challenge now is to truly optimise it, to make sure that the right people are in the right roles doing the right things!

So what is best practice in terms of skills and capabilities? What should this "right team" look like? What are the core jobs and what should those people be focussing on and delivering?

Research is showing that to build a truly effective and powerful e-commerce team, it needs to have 3 core roles at its heart. These 3 roles are the main pillars that will support the whole customer engagement effort and around which the rest of the organisation can be established.

These 3 would report into the Head of e-Commerce and would be key members of the leadership team. They represent the core steps in the value chain, put simply: *get customers, get them to buy, get them to come back!*

★ *Head of Customer Acquisition*
★ *Head of Customer Conversion*
★ *Head of Customer Retention*

Each of these three should be the 3 key hires for any e-commerce organisation. No matter what decisions are made about outsourcing and working with vendors and partners, there needs to be this kind of dedicated focus and skill in-house to take ownership and drive for results. In small or start-up situations, these 3 people would be responsible for a wide range of activities and initiatives and would need to have the experience to prioritise hard as to where best to allocate time and resource. As the business builds so these 3 would naturally bring in expert managers and juniors who would report to them and take on more specific areas of activity.

We can consider in this chapter the following points:

i.   What is each of the 3 specifically responsible for?
ii. What are their core metrics /deliverables?
iii. What are the key skills /experience they need to have?
iv. What are the other core functions that need to be part of the e-commerce team?
v.   What overall management team is required?
vi. What size should the team be in total?
vii. What's the key to making the right level of investment in skills and people?
viii. A short case study /example

First then, what is each of these 3 responsible for?

★ **Head of Customer Acquisition:**

- Paid Search
- SEO
- Affiliates
- Online marketing (which could include campaigns, advertising, email)
- Social media (content development, content distribution and PR)
- Mobile apps development

Key deliverables/metrics:
- *# of visitors*
- *cost /visit*

★ Head of Customer Conversion:

- User experience
- Market and customer insight
- IA (information architecture)
- site analytics
- design + layout
- functionality, user tools, recommendations etc

Key deliverables/metrics:
- *% conversion visitors to sales*
- *average basket /order size £*

★ Head of Customer Retention:

- database development
- Email marketing
- CRM *(contact strategy, contact programme, loyalty incentives, loyalty partners)*

Key deliverables /metrics:
- *% repeat visitors*
- *% repeat purchasers*

iii. These 3 function /team heads need to have the following skills and experiences:

    i. Significant experience in e-commerce: at least 3 years working in an online transaction environment

    ii. Broad expertise in the specific core area: so for example the Head of Customer Acquisition must have experience not just in Search but across some /all of the other main elements too

    iii. Digital know-how: have knowledge /ideally expertise in all digital channels so online, mobile and also interactive TV (expected to develop further in 2013)

iv. Multi-channel savvy: in many companies, digital channels need to work alongside the Store or Call Centre Operations team to drive complimentary activity and customer engagement

v. Entrepreneurial mind-set: e-commerce generally is still in a high growth phase, it is changing fast, there is need for constant innovation and improvement, structures and processes are not mature, there's plenty of market share to go for! So these people need to have that self-starting hunger and desire, they will need to be able to set their own agenda, they will need to have the determination to constantly improve the customer experience.

iv. For an e-commerce team to be complete, there are 3 other functions that need to be managed and led. In a Retail market, these are:

- Buying and Merchandising
- Technology
- Fulfilment

These are treated separately because (i) all retailers will often have teams in these areas which can, at least initially, take on the additional e-commerce sales channels as well, and (ii) Technology and Fulfilment for an e-commerce operation can be outsourced. In such circumstances there might need to be an Operations Head on the team in-house who can oversee and manage the outsourcing suppliers but it does potentially remove the need to build and own larger teams.

In Technology, there are a growing number of increasingly sophisticated "white label" outsourced platform providers who can provide the e-commerce backbone. Companies like Venda, who work with TK Maxx, Orange, Wickes, Monsoon, Superdrug and others. Or eCommera, who work with the likes of House of Fraser, Asda, Hamleys and Space.NK. These and other organisations like them have scalable and flexible solutions that enable companies to essentially pay as they go and avoid the substantial risk and cost of building their own.

In Fulfilment, there are out-sourcing companies which range from Royal Mail and UPS to dedicated e-commerce providers like iForce who work with major supermarket chains like Waitrose and Sainsbury's, GSI who work with Ralph Lauren, Timberland and Dockers and 3P Logistics who fulfil for the likes of Morrisons and the Fashion Hut.

v. In summary, an e-commerce leadership team might naturally look like this:

Head of / Director of e-Commerce

▼

Customer Acquisition	Customer Conversion	Customer Retention	Operations
–	–	–	–
–	–	–	–
–	–	–	–

As mentioned, depending on the outsourcing strategy Operations may be split between a Technology Head and a Fulfillment Head. And depending on the size and scale of the business, there might be a separate online Merchandising team.

vi. Size of team will naturally be driven by the amount of revenue and profit being generated. But there is some investment and risk required at various stages, especially while the business is in its early phases. Many e-commerce operators, especially in today's economic climate, are cautious and would prefer to invest and build behind the revenue, let the business cash flow enable it and then we'll put in the extra resource.

But this is a high growth fast-changing more entrepreneurial environment, and many businesses remain stuck at a certain level unable to really break-through to the next stage of sales growth they aspire to. Often it is not the consumer proposition which is out of sync but simply there isn't the right and sufficient dedicated skills and resources in place to drive this and make this change.

That is why this note talks about the 3 core pillars. Without these 3 people a business will never fulfil its potential; it will never make the break-throughs necessary to get to that next level of customer engagement and experience.

vii. Where there is hesitation, where there is uncertainty about investment in people and resources, then there is one key that can unlock the potential. That is analytics:

Today, there is a superb array of web analytic tools, many available for free, which will give tremendous insight into the potential of the business.

Many e-commerce businesses get lots of visitors but simply do not convert them into customers. Thousands of people may see the site but only a handful may buy. And many more will never come back. Basic analysis will show why these visitors do not buy. It will show what they do when they arrive, what they look at and at what point they leave. It will show the number of "unfinished check-outs", the number of uncompleted registrations, the % who never progress beyond the first page. It will show where they come from and what sources are driving traffic, and which are not. It can give demographic insight, whether people enjoy and would recommend the site and show the strength of positive and negative sentiment toward the overall online experience

The book *"e-Shock 2020"* shows a 6 step test that can give this insight. And all the analytic tools described there are available for free.

What it can show is what's missing, what revenues could be generated if the problem areas were addressed, if the conversion ratio was closer to best practice, if the customer experience was optimised. That will show the potential ROI; the return a business can get if it has the people and resource to go after these problem areas and turn them into practicable and realisable opportunities. That can be the key, the catalyst. That can help persuade a board of investors to take that next step, bring in the right people, staff up the 3 Pillars, because the size of the prize can be quantified and measured and the return can be captured.

viii. Zulily.com. We have described their remarkable progress elsewhere, but what do they believe has been the key to their success?

How has it made that leap in organisation size and growth and done it so quickly?

The key is that the founders are analytic fanatics. They pour over the numbers, they analyse site performance, they are constantly identifying new ways to optimise performance, to tweak up the sales conversion ratio, to push up average basket size, to increase the % of repeat purchases. The analytics can clearly demonstrate that if they make a change here its impact on sales can be quantified. It gives them and the investors the confidence to bring in new people, to get that dedicated eg user experience expert, to staff up the "3 Pillars", to target and go after the ROI, to provide the skills and the resources to capture that latent value and help build and drive the business to the next stage.

Chapter 12

Building a Leading e-Commerce Business

How to Establish the "Virtuous Cycle" of Sustainable Self-Funding Growth and Development

Here is a common story I hear: "everyone speaks about the opportunity in digital and e-commerce, and I'm sure we could build out successful new revenue streams. But it all comes down to investment, and often requests for substantial investment. Each business has plans to hire people, build tech platforms, add to marketing costs yet it's all based on guesstimates and forecasts and they may be too optimistic. Is there another way to develop this area while managing the up-front costs and investment risk"?

The answer is that there is another way and one which is potentially a lot easier. And it is *self-funding*. It simply provides a sustainable way to maximise the growth in the e-commerce operation. And in doing so generate additional streams of revenue, and profit, that can be used to justify continued investment.

This alternative approach is the "Virtuous Cycle of e-Commerce investment". It consists of just three keys. And it's all about having the right people in place. The business needs just 3 key people: a Head of Conversion, a Manager of Analytics and a Web Master. These 3 work "hand-in-glove" to create a virtuous cycle of activity.

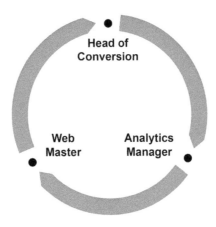

1. The Head of Conversion

This person is responsible for converting traffic to sales. They are not involved in acquiring traffic. They are not a Search /PPC /Affiliates expert. They are however insiders, looking at what happens at the next stage of the value chain. Once we've got the traffic what are we doing with them?

Their key remit is looking at the web site /user experience. They are the ones who are constantly examining the site information architecture, the layout of the content, the look and feel of the web site, the whole end-to-end user experience. What happens to people once they arrive>? What parts of the online store do they visit? And what parts never seem to get many visitors. How long do people stay? What engages them and what puts them off? How many put items in a basket, and how many never complete that basket, what if we change this instruction or make this process shorter or skip this section or put this button in highlights, does any of that make a difference?

At the end of the day this is in many ways the key role in an e-commerce organisation, and it needs someone dedicated to this task. Someone who has only one very clear metric and focus in mind. What is the % conversion ratio? And yes, there are subsidiary ratios such as average basket size and ave. number of items ordered. But visits: sales is the key.

And yet most e-commerce operations do *not* have one of these people. This key role is often subsumed within a broader role of Online Marketing Manager or Web Site Manager. And as a result the focus is often lost. And often, not surprisingly visits: sales ratios are not as leveraged as they could /should be.

2. Analytics Manager

This person is one of the two key partners to our Head of Conversion. This person is in charge of all the data. They have been tasked to ensure that there is a proper and effective web analytics process and data-gathering capability in place. And their task is to provide the analysis and insight that can show what improvements can be made.

They have the opportunity to provide the *weekly or even daily change agenda*. They should be in a position to know where each visitor goes and where they fall away. There is the classic waterfall analysis that shows for each 100 visitors how many make it all the way though to check-out and purchase? How many does the site lose even at the home page? How many get to the registration page for example and drop out there? How many baskets are set-up and left uncompleted?

And if these Analytics Managers are in any way curious they will be not just the analysers of the data. But they will be the interrogators too! They will want to understand why it is that people drop out or don't complete? They will want to be holding regular focus groups and pieces of research to ask visitors: what went wrong, why did you not complete, and most importantly what could we have done differently that would have made your experience easier, better, more enjoyable, more convenient, simpler, more compelling so that you would have completed?

And they would also be constantly reviewing best practices and asking why can't we match them? So everyone knows and talks about Amazon's One Click ordering process for example. But how many companies offer that facility aside from Amazon? Here we are some 10 years on from when that simple but powerful piece of functionality was first introduced. But how few today copy or offer that? But the technology to do it is now straightforward, as many web site platforms do offer the facility to save credit card details for future ordering. But where is the One Click button?

3. The Web Master

So we have the Conversion head who is orchestrating and driving to generate higher sales from the marketing and online activity. We have the analytics and insight that shows what can be improved and where the key opportunities lie. Now all we need is the final piece of the jigsaw.

And this is the Web Master. This person is the one who implements the technical changes that have been identified. It's about working closely with the Conversion Manager to identify the highest priorities for change, the items that will make the biggest differences to sales.

They then have the technical capability and importantly, the access, to make those changes to the site. Oftentimes this may be simple changes to content or moving layout or information or making some things more prominent or reducing the number of pre-registration questions or adding in a piece of functionality. Each item may in itself be quite small but its impact can be quite high. Many are the stories of eg moving a Next Step button above the fold and seeing basket completion jump by 20%.

But what is key here, is that this Web Master has access. This person needs to have the agility to get to the source code and the authority to change things. What this needs to avoid, and it's situation which is very common today, where the e-commerce team want to make changes requiring technical input and then they get told that they will have to wait for IT team resource, that there is a queue of projects from across the whole company waiting to be implemented, that this e-commerce initiative will have to wait till resource can be allocated and found. And oh, by the way, that will be in 6 month's time.

What this Web Master also needs is the skill to think and act quickly and entrepreneurially. What shortcut might exist that could enable this change to be made easily? Is there already a piece of eg Open Source software ready developed that could perhaps be adapted and deployed. Is there some solution in the Cloud that might enable this problem to be outsourced or solved in a different way?

What is key is that the tasks and changes need to be done quickly. They cannot sit in a 6 month queue. E-Commerce as indeed all technology today does not sit in traditional legacy system lead times. Things are moving at such a pace that they need to be captured now!

Implications and Conclusion

Achieving this virtuous cycle is not hard. It's mostly about formalising and focusing current resources onto these key priorities. Such people also need not be high cost and often young rising stars with a few years good online and e-commerce experience should be able to adapt and respond to the challenge.

The main process change is enabling a Web Master to have access and authority. That may require the approval of the Senior IT Director and may require some initial partnering and working with the IT team to ensure good governance and safe management. But again it should not be difficult to achieve.

What is clear is that the best e-commerce sites are achieving very high growth rates, they are hitting that virtuous cycle where not only can they make changes quickly internally but their success reaches out and creates that buzz and excitement that makes a difference, that gets people talking about the business, that encourages more visitors and gets more recommendations from friends, family and supporters.

Key is that change and enhancement can happen in near real time. There need be no delay. The analysis does not need to wait for eg the weekly trading meeting. It does not wait for an IT team to decide when and if it will make changes. The whole visit to sale conversion experience is being constantly and continuously optimised. And in this way a company can ensure that the visitor experience is enjoyable and easy, that customer satisfaction is at its highest, that problems are identified and resolved immediately, that sales and revenues are maximised!

Chapter 13

Digital Evolution of Marketing/Marketing Department Organisation Structures

1. Background

In the good old days! Marketing was relatively straightforward to organise. Back in the 1970's when the marketing function really began to gain widespread recognition and adoption, there were typically just a few key levers that the department was responsible for. And these were mostly around building brand awareness among the target customer/consumer group.

Today's world however has become infinitely more challenging and complex. The role and responsibility of marketing has grown significantly. Companies today now almost universally look to their marketing team as their engine of growth. Market sectors are more competitive, they are usually global, they have become multi-channel, technology is proving disruptive while at the same time being attractive, expertise eg in mobile, social, SEO is becoming more specialist and harder to obtain…getting any increase in market share and gains in revenue is just more challenging.

The progressive marketing function however is now looking to tackle these challenges head-on. They are taking responsibility for developing the company's strategy and plans that can navigate through this market maze and develop winning solutions. The need for an integrated, multi-channel, technically literate, innovative and ever more entrepreneurial team is now becoming paramount.

This chapter looks at the evolution of the marketing organisation. It starts with "the good old days" and looks at where things now are. There is no "right/proven" structure and model. Every company of course is different. There are differences in B2B and B2C (principally B2B sometimes have less "digitally" sophisticated and developed customers) and companies are very influenced by number of products/number of Brands, number of countries sold to, size of revenue streams, readiness of the senior directors/officers of the company to invest, how responsive the business is to emerging new channels of communication like web, mobile, social, and just how challenging the marketing team wants to be.

2. The good old days.

There were principally two key levers: Promotions and Advertising.

The Proms team developed the annual plan and set out the promotions cycle. They would agree plans with Sales dept. about what sort of incentives required at different stage of the sales cycle. Activity would be driven mostly by the Sales team and the needs of key Trading customers. So there would be something planned for each quarter. The range of options was fairly basic, choose from direct mail, sampling, discounts and if possible eg "on-pack" competitions.

Alongside this and in support would be the *Product /Brand advertising*. This would depend on budgets and would be all about building awareness and recognition. It might be on TV or in Print or on the Radio. (Media buying and planning would invariably be outsourced to the Ad agency)

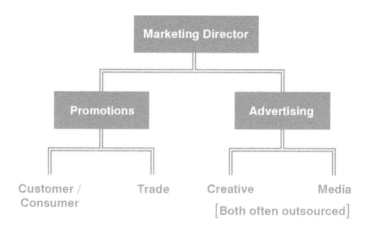

3. The 1990's

Still before the real commercial advent of the internet, yet Marketing even at this point was becoming significantly more sophisticated. The catalyst here was the availability of data and more and more computer processing power available on the desktop. Suddenly a marketing team could recruit in a data /insight /research team who could analyse customer behaviour, spot trends, engage in richer and deeper segmentation and identify much more tailored and refined and sophisticated marketing campaigns and activities.

So marketing teams might typically have a Head of Insight (in early days this might have been the Market Research Mgr), who would take responsibility for data and analytics. The work might be outsourced to a specialist data/research team or combined with some in-house expertise.

In addition, the whole concept of the "Brand" began to take root. Brand Mgrs. began to proliferate as companies looked at the pioneer of effective Brand marketing, Procter & Gamble, and wanted to adopt and copy their, it seemed, proven success model. Brand Mgrs. were charged with being the "guardians of the brand". While no-one was quite sure what that meant! it seemed mostly about measuring and monitoring Brand awareness, propensity to purchase and brand sentiment. It also meant being the champion of the brand internally across the company. That usually also meant being the coordinator of brand planning, brand budgets, brand promotions, brand development and brand advertising. And in some instances having those skills reporting directly into them rather than being separated out.

But this era did particularly herald a step-change in the profile and power of Marketing. Marketing Directors began to appear on the main board. The Brand Mgr started to become a powerful figure of influence and responsibility. The team became more than just administrators of a promotions budget. They became responsible formally with Sales for top line revenue growth, and often took on the Brand/Product P&L. They also had a much more involved role in the long term. No longer just about short term tactical campaigns and quarterly sales programmes. There was now also a key responsibility to use the data and insight to generate product development programmes which would keep the Brand alive and contemporary and compelling.

3. Now!

Today's world has seen a step change in complexity. We now live in this multi-channel, technology-enabled world of innovation, new ideas and constant change. Channels to market have proliferated and fragmented. It's no longer a simple world of TV, Print, Radio. Now add of course so much more whether via mobile, tablet, webcast, YouTube, Pinterest, Facebook, Twitter, social media monitoring generally, in-game advertising, pre-roll, SEO, SEM, blogs, eCRM, e-Commerce…the list goes on.

And yet, this has all fallen to the Marketing Department. No other team has stood up and tried to take this all on board. And typically no other team in the company would naturally have the skills or market understanding to adopt and embrace all this change and opportunity. So everyone now looks to Marketing. Tell us about these changing market/multi-channel/omni-channel conditions, how do we now reach out to our target audience (they are no longer where they used to be!), get us the data and insight that enables us to understand what marketing communications will work and what will not, conduct the tests that show how to engage with our target customers in this digital world, identify the new programmes and activities and product development which will ensure we remain/become successful!

No small challenge.

And so the Marketing department has had to evolve rapidly. It has had to take on and recruit new skills/ new people. It has had to expand simply to cover the basics. It now is expected to have skills in all these "new" areas and to understand mobile, social, Twitter etc etc. Over the course of the past decade marketing teams have grown in numbers (though not necessarily in comms spending budgets) and have become even more "centre stage". They are now the champions of not just the Brand, but also of the Customer. They now formulate the total customer engagement strategy. Instead of Sales driving Marketing (as used to happen), it's now the other way round. Marketing are the key. They are the ones who are at the heart of the business. It is their knowledge about digital and the changing market environment that is dictating the whole organisation's future strategy. It is now Marketing's relationship with IT that is the core team dynamic. It is how those two departments operate and collaborate and work effectively together that will ultimately decide who will be the winners by 2020.

So in the next two diagrams/org structures, the first illustration shows how the Marketing skills set has proliferated and the range of new skills and functions the team had to adopt. The second chart shows how the better Marketing departments have come to terms with this, how they have reorganised to manage that proliferation to find a new simpler more streamlined more manageable and more effective org.solution.

As mentioned at the beginning of this note, there are no "right answers". And this has simply tried to show how things have changed, and by just how much! And what some possible ways of navigating the organisation through this changing dynamic period might look like.

i.   Extended Marketing value chain /org.:

(ii) a Streamlined /consolidated Marketing organisation structure:

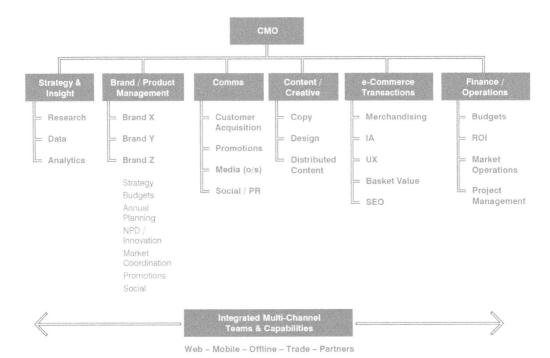

Chapter 14

Multi-National Marketing: Impact of Digital on Organisation Structures

Against the global background of digital innovation and transformation, Marketing is facing its own challenges. The move to a multi-channel /omni-channel world is changing the whole marketing mix and requiring investment in new skills, technical literacy and ways of understanding what customers will best respond to. Whether Business or Consumer, expectations are the same: customers are increasingly demanding self-serve value and convenience.

So how for example should a Marketing team organise itself to meet this fast-changing environment? For sure they do need "digital skills", they do need people who really get this "new marketing agenda" and have the know-how, best practices, war stories and lessons learned of what works, and what does not! But Marketing also needs to find ways to integrate these skills and organise so it can embrace them.

The challenge is that most companies of course do not start with a blank sheet of paper. They do have existing system and processes, they have teams who have worked with them often for many years, they may be global in span and operation, they will have other demands and priorities on their time, not all their customers will want digital comms and interaction, not all their teams will know how to start testing out and exploring the digital agenda.

Because of this most companies will often start by appointing eg a "Chief Digital Officer". This is someone who is the champion of all things digital. This is an educator, an informer, a voice of influence, a home of best practice, a driver of change. Often this person will recruit a small team of like-minded digital experts who can spread the net wider. This team too will often take on specific responsibilities, pilot new ideas, establish platforms eg in e-commerce, build key relationships with agencies and third party providers in this space. They will also typically encourage local teams in international markets to establish their own in-house digital capability. This enables the digital team and capability to grow more quickly and builds a network of key local "in-brand" /in-house digital advocates.

At some point this network will grow so that we see the beginnings of a "hub and spoke" model. That is a core digital expert team at the centre continuing to push the digital strategy, testing new opportunities and supplemented by "spokes", key talent in local subsidiary business units who take charge of local digital tactics and implementation. This might especially be around Search marketing, local advertising, local online promotions etc.

Some key questions can be identified which might influence and drive how this "hub and spoke" model might take shape for an organisation: it's a digital marketing structure test.

Digital Marketing: 6 keys questions to determine how to organise at a multi-national level?

1. *What is current infrastructure?*
   - number of people
   - where they are located /number of different locations
   - what sort of skills

2. *How many Brands with online potential?*
   -number of brands with multi-country reach
   -demand for digital for each /variation by country

3. *Current status of each Brand /in each key national market*
   - has own online site today?
   - amount of traffic /visitors?
   - the Brand's desire to use online to grow the business?
   - e-commerce potential?

4. *What's the potential multi-country reach?*
   - how many brands have a multi-country audience and reach today?
   - what's the potential?
   - do they all aspire to be global?

5. *Current structure*
   - who is responsible for Online /Digital today?
   - any central control or all distributed around the businesses
   - who has more control /influence in this area: IT or Marketing or Group

> *6. What KPI if any exist today around brand marketing effectiveness?*
>   - is culture /control driven from the centre or it dispersed /localised?
>   - how are brands measuring digital interest and demand?

Developing some understanding of each company's situation can help define the hub and spoke model and determine what key skills and responsibilities should be established where.

It is possible to consider some radical options such as everything digital is outsourced, or everything is centralised in a hub or everything is decentralised into local markets. There is no "right" or "wrong answer", what works for one organisation may not work for another and any solution needs to fit company culture, readiness for change, how demanding for digital are its customers, amount of resource and investment available and how passionate and committed to "digital" are the senior management of the company. But certainly the model that most organisations are working with today is some variation on a hub and spoke model.

Digital organisation options:

i.   In-house vs. Outsource

ii. All centrally located /controlled:
     -"a centre of excellence"
     - managing all strategy, planning and administering all local execution
     This avoids duplication of resource and effort and each local market "reinventing the wheel" for itself and perhaps making the same mistakes.

iii. All distributed to the spokes
     This provides stronger local ownership but likely leads to duplication of cost and also of resource, disparate and sometimes confusing presentation of the Brand, no coordinated marketing, different customer experiences which may lead also to disappointment and loss of engagement.

iv. Hub 'n Spoke
     Spoke could include:
     ★ local national Customer Acquisition:
         - Search, both SEO and SEM,
         - local partnerships

        - local affiliates
        - local content and updating
        - local store finder
        - any click n' reserve /click n'collect solutions
★ Customer services
★ Fulfilment /delivery

Customer Acquisition could start in Hub in initial phases till reach local scale

Hub could include:
★ all Technology
        - e-commerce platform
        - Web Master
        - Mobile developments /apps

★ all Customer Analytics /Conversion
        - UX
        - design
        - analytics

★ all Customer Retention
        - CRM software eg Salesforce.com
        - Data analysis /segmentation /data insight

★ Social Media
        - this can be critical to control, monitor and influence in coordinated and consistent way what is said about a global /international brand and to manage its online reputation.

★★★★★

This whole area of how to organise in Marketing to facilitate and enable the most effective marketing to customers is a big topic and this note can only begin to set out some of the challenges and options.

    This same set of issues is also very relevant to IT. How Marketing is organised needs to also reflect any developments and change to the company's technology team structures. And if "hub and spoke" is an appropriate framework for the Marketing team then it's likely that the same market and customer drivers should indicate the direction that IT should also be organising around.

Most companies will typically start to address these challenges by establishing a "Digital Steering Committee". This group will be made up of all key stakeholders and likely include the CMO, the CTO and head of key Brands or Business Units. A common solution can be identified that can work at least for the core brands and businesses to start with. What is critical to recognise is that any solution must be regularly reviewed and checked that it is still appropriate. This digital world is of course moving so quickly that what is right for today may not suit the company as it evolves and reaches higher levels of digital maturity.

Chapter 15

Omni vs. Multi

There's lots of "digital jargon" out there and one concept often discussed is "omni-channel". This new phrase has emerged and is being touted as "the next big trend". It's especially relevant to the Retail industry but in fact applies to any organisation supplying, distributing or otherwise interacting with customers across multiple touch points and different channels on and off line.

Some commentators suggest that "omni-channel" is something different to "multi-channel", which was "last year's" hot topic. But is there a difference really? Aren't we all in effect saying the same thing? Simply that in this fast-changing world where digital technology is challenging traditional ways of customer engagement, that to be successful, then for example a retail group needs to operate effectively across *all* channels, whether it's store, online, mobile, TV or whichever medium the customer is interested in buying. And surely we all get that nowadays, don't we? We've seen the stats, we've experienced the sea-change in consumer habits and preferences, we know surely that to be successful that this is the new game in town and one we need to learn to play.

And while all that's right, it's worth just stopping and reflecting on why this new term "omni" has arisen, why are we being confronted with yet new concepts and challenges, as if the day job isn't demanding enough already!

The answer is because for many, "multi-channel" has actually meant not much more than just the e-commerce /online route to market. Companies have hired "multi-channel" directors where their remit is very simply to head up that new channel, e-commerce, and drive sales online. Their task is to build the digital flagship", to develop engagement with customers in that arena specifically. If there is any "multi-channel" responsibility it's often just about making sure that eg the web site address is on the shopping bag, or the TV ad refers to the web site or that there is a store locator function on the web homepage. Multi has typically meant a focus online with maybe a measure of marketing connectivity that offers some apparent cross-platform communication to customers.

But of course the cross-platform opportunity is bigger than that. And this is where it starts to become difficult. There is the bigger opportunity to provide a unified customer experience. And that means that whatever channel the customer touches they will see the same stock at the same price with the same promotions merchandised in the same way and that connection is made and updated in real time.

That is not easy to do. And that is why for many companies, "multi-channel" has stopped at doing "simple connected marketing". And why most companies have not yet got to that broader "omni" capability. But that omni-capability is worth so much more, that ability to truly engage with customers no matter what the channel and yet provide a seamless and integrated and updated experience.

Let's look at a case study. Aurora Fashions is perhaps an unlikely but certainly excellent example of a retail group who have gone beyond "multi" and embraced "omni". It's been a challenging journey which has taken time and commitment as well as establishing a far-reaching vision of the benefits and business gain to be had.

Aurora Fashions case study

About 6 years ago, they embarked on their multi-channel journey. Their mission was to be able to do business with their customers "Anywhere and Everywhere". To challenge themselves and to differentiate their mission from the general multichannel talk, they set their sights on delivering the "Omni-channel" experience.

Aurora runs 4 key retail chains. They are Oasis, Coast, Warehouse and Karen Millen. Their IT Director who kick-started this initiative was John Bovill. He was an early advocate and believed that, get this right, and it would not be about cannibalising existing store sales, but quite the contrary, it would be a net driver of sales growth and competitive advantage.

While the early phases of John's journey were to establish the basic functioning of the key transaction web sites, it quickly became clear that as online sales grew so that success also created a problem. How could an online consumer tell if an item was actually in-stock, what if they bought the item online but then the fulfilment team found that the item had been sold, how could Aurora in effect provide some kind-of real time inventory system that would automatically update and so show only what's available, and could they also provide this same system in-store so shop assistants in Southampton could find an item in a store in Aberdeen, and could all this be done in an accurate, up-to-the-minute way so that stores, shoppers and Aurora warehousing and distribution staff could all react immediately and efficiently. And if all that was done, could it be implemented and deployed in such a way that it would in fact drive incremental sales and provide that better and unified customer experience?

Aurora set about that task and it required a major systems alignment and transformation. They appointed Ish Patel as their "Omni-channel director" to coordinate and lead this real –time multi-channel upgrade, they committed significant time and energy to explaining and training so that staff throughout the group would understand and most importantly be able to use the system solution in the way it was envisaged.

And this has now been achieved. Digital commerce has been merged with physical retailing to create a seamless experience for the customer. It has established a new model for stock management as it opens up the whole stock inventory across the full store portfolio. "With our Anywhere Everywhere model, we are saying to customers that if we have it in the UK, then we will get it to you wherever you want it". This is not just true for shoppers online but also for every store. "Every store now has the opportunity to boost sales by fulfilling web orders. It also enables even the smallest store to have access to the Brand's full product range, even to the limited editions".

Stock records are updated in real time. The old approach of updating every 24 hrs is now seen as "dinosaur territory". There is now "seamless integration" throughout the supply chain from Merchandising, Warehousing, Store, Sales analytics, Planning, Customer Services, and Fulfilment. What's more to really drive through the benefits of this, Aurora promise to their customers that they will deliver stock from the store within 90 minutes if the consumer lives in the same town as the stock item is found.

This has led to a 28% uplift in availability of online products and has begun to materially drive extra sales. Online conversion rates doubled. The early metrics showed 10 to 15% uplift in like-for like sales. What's more and what was not expected is that the system enables Aurora to maximise its full price sales. "In some instances full price sales have risen by 80% to 98%. We find we can use this system to highlight product availability and make sure that demand is met and not disappointed. We can be sure therefore to fulfil and every product line gets maximum exposure because it's available "everywhere!"

Store staff have become real enthusiasts as they get credit for the additional sales they can generate through their finding stock for their customers or for assisting in the follow-up local deliveries. Now moving forward, fixed tills are being replaced by iPads which shop assistants carry around with them, "It's more fun, it's much

> *more exciting, it gives us a lot bigger role…our single view of stock is very much underpinning how we now move forward". And it has become a hallmark also supporting the company's international expansion.*

Aurora has been a pioneer, but others are fast catching-up. House of Fraser, Debenhams, Tesco, John Lewis are all vanguard organisations pushing out this omni-channel capability.

Marks and Spencer is said to have invested > £500m in its multi-channel "foundation programme" to also create this single view of stock no matter what the channel in real time. For sure it's not an easy thing to deliver but as others follow Aurora's lead it is clear that "omni-channel" is going to be the way of commerce in the future.

What does this mean for retail and other groups as they start to build their own omni-channel group? What sort of people and skills should they be searching for? Aurora has approached this from an IT /Technical perspective aligning internal systems to present this single view of stock to the customer. And that is without doubt one critical dimension. It's also important that the Marketing Chief is able to match this and in parallel ensure that this integrated internal view is captured and communicated in the most powerful and effective way to the consumer. And with that in mind the marketing team needs to adopt the sort of profile described in this extract from a recent job description and candidate search:

The multi-channel Marketing Director: Job description

> *The Marketing Director needs to have a <u>truly</u> Multi-channel outlook and perspective. They must be "the voice of the customer" no matter which way the customer connects with us. This person is the overall champion of the customer experience and has responsibility for ensuring that experience is fully integrated. This means in practice that whether a customer interacts in-store, by phone or online they will see, hear and feel the same thing. All marketing communication needs to be "joined-up" and planned to be complementary and supportive and timely. The customer needs to be comfortable and confident in whatever way they choose to browse or buy. The customer must see the same stock, the same availability, be empowered to eg "phone and reserve" or "click and collect", the pricing and merchandising and special offers must be aligned and the same, they must be able to see their account history no matter which way they have purchased in the past and the Company must be able to recognise and deliver that.*

> *This role is an important step in the Company's journey to deliver a fully integrated, joined-up customer experience. The multi-channel Marketing director must be the champion of this journey. Success will be delivered by reference to specific customer satisfaction scores, increased transaction size and specifically targeted revenue increases.*

Retail Week conferences often feature a number of speeches and agenda items on this multi vs. omni theme and it's clearly something that retailers want to explore and find out more. But the key message is that "omni" is useful as a concept to show there is further to go than just the "multi" solution and that true joined-up and integrated customer engagement is yet a step further on this digital journey. For sure it is more challenging and will require more far-reaching change but it is a path that others have shown is possible and it is a path that can produce significant benefits. Without doubt, the winning organisations of tomorrow will be those who have really embraced what this omni-channel world now demands!

Chapter 16

How to Capture the "Digital Opportunity"?
An alternative organisation /operating solution

Most every company today is looking at the Digital world and wondering how best to take advantage. Many look enviously at pure plays and start-ups who are unencumbered by legacy systems and historic ways of working and who seem to be able to make quick and rapid progress, have flexibility to adapt and change and seem able to capture new market opportunities so readily. Meantime, the more established continue to struggle with change.

So is there another way? Is the pursuit of "digital" to remain a constant uphill battle fighting for resource and budget? Or is there perhaps another route, one that respects and understands that the core business must adapt but necessarily will need to move at a certain pace and timetable only, that legacy systems will take time to update and upgrade and that while there is a digitised end-game in place it will be something that may take several years rather than several months to accomplish.

The answer is that there is another path that an organisation can pursue. And it can unleash tremendous energy and opportunity. Let's consider a few examples:

Barclaycard*:* part of Barclays Bank and increasingly seen as the "the innovation arm of the Bank. Barclaycard was determined to take advantage of and exploit digital opportunities. While the core business started taking the usual steps around "digital transformation", they realised that their "bottom-up" change approach would be painstaking and take time. It meant gradually training existing staff with new skills, bringing in selected individuals into key posts to act as catalysts and "transformers" who could champion the digital agenda, launching and relaunching the key web sites to better showcase products and services…but all to an agenda that had to work with a "business as usual" methodology that allowed existing ways of working to continue and gradually adapt.

So what did Barclaycard do? They set up a separate stand-alone e-Ventures unit. Thy realised that they had a unique asset which was having strong commercial arrangements already in place with just about every merchant and retailer in the UK. How leverage that? Imagine, they said, if we had a clean sheet of paper today, how would we leverage our assets and partnerships? What could we do to leverage that in this digital world, without having to worry about legacy and change and old ideas and ways of working? What would that new found freedom enable us to do?

So Barclaycard have set up a stand-alone business called Digital Marketplace. The plan is to launch a number of new and separate businesses. The first is called Bespoke Offers. It offers daily deals and discounts that leverage those retailer relationships. So find discounts off eg Marks and Spencer, or cheap holiday deals or vouchers /money off hotels and restaurants.

www.bespokeoffers.co.uk is not the only daily deals business in the market place but it is the only one that has those already established commercial partnerships that it can leverage to get the best deals or the most exclusive offers.

Under the leadership of CEO David Herrick the team was quickly built. It has its own space, technology, culture and resources all dedicated to this venture. It means they can build quickly and establish an entrepreneurial culture that is self-starting and wants to work in agile fashion and achieve on very fast time-frames. It is in effect a dot.com style business but with the backing and leverage of a very established parent corporation.

Homeserve: Homeserve is a FTSE 250 plc operating internationally and providing home emergency repair and insurance services. They have major long term affinity relationships with Utility companies and appliance manufacturers. They have grown from small start-up beginnings to a more than £1bn market cap over the past 20 years and have always had an inherently entrepreneurial streak in their culture and make-up. But a £1bn market cap company, even with "just" 20 years of being, still has its legacy environment and business as usual needs and practices. So the CEO, Richard Harpin, who has built-up and led the company for its 20 year history started to ask the question about how better to take advantage of new digital technologies, tools and ways of working. Sure the core business needs to go through its own "digital transformation" but meantime, while that will take time, what else can Homeserve plc achieve?

So they, like Barclaycard, have set up a stand-alone e-Ventures unit. Their key question was: if we were building Homeserve from scratch today, in this new digital world, what would we do and how would we do it? What business model would we adopt that would exploit digital but perhaps do so in a different style from the way Homeserve plc was built up?

This e-Ventures unit is called Homeserve Alliance. It understands that one of the great advantages that digital brings is new and more powerful ways to connect businesses together. Whether we call it "social media" or perhaps more simply establishing communities of shared interest, the digital world enables new connections to be formed very quickly and very efficiently.

Homeserve Alliance is an alliance of small to mid-sized home emergency repair companies across the UK. Homeserve have targeted what they feel is the top 100 such companies, all independents, all keen to grow more themselves, and and with the aim to give each an exclusive local territory. The idea is to work with each to provide consumers with this network of the best home repair companies in their area. The consumer will have a clear portal and start point to find the best local provider. And at the same time, Homeserve will work with each provider to establish a strong network and UK franchise. In particular each local firm that's been chosen was keen to take more advantage of digital to grow their business but lacked the scale and so the resources themselves on their own to fund eg better web site development, more effective Search capabilities or more online marketing. Homeserve will now fund that and can use a templated approach to roll out local marketing campaigns for each provider in a more cost-effective way.

The win-wins here are that the local provider gets a turbo-charge to its growth ambitions through much more powerful digital marketing, the consumer gets a trusted local provider whose service levels are overseen by the Homeserve team and Homeserve itself gets a share of the incremental revenues that the local provider gets. An early example of just how successful this is proving to be has been the work achieved with local Yorkshire independent Safegas. Homeserve worked with Safegas to redo the web site, reorganise their SEO and SEM and set up a strong customer contact email marketing program. By the end of the first year, www.safegas.co.uk was seeing a near 30% uplift in sales and a growing recognition for being the No.1 provider in its area.

In addition Homeserve is learning. It is learning about new digital tools and approaches. It is learning about how to exploit these new market place opportunities. It can second people from the core PLC business so they can see and find out and contribute first-hand to the development of the Alliance venture. They can then, hopefully, transfer ways of thinking and working with speed and challenge back to the parent company. Another win?

Barclaycard and Homeserve are but two examples of companies taking advantage of digital in this way. Intel and Unilever have both been operating an e-Ventures division for more than 10 years and have gained a substantial amount of experience through that.

Unilever for example currently has some 10 different businesses which it has either started itself or invested significantly in. One such business is Brandtone, which is pioneering new ways of using mobile phone technology in fast growing consumer markets including South Africa, Brazil, Russia, India and China. Brandtone partners with leading brands to profile consumers, collect data and target marketing for their products and promotions. Unilever sponsored and backed the founding management team.

Given that Unilever has been vested in this way of developing business for some years it has also achieved some substantial successes. One such is BrainJuicer.com. They are a market research consultancy using new technology to apply psychology, behavioural economics and social sciences to better predict human behaviour. They have built up a reputation as a thought leader and change agent. Unilever Ventures invested in BrainJuicer.com in its very early start-up days. The company was IPO'd and then subsequently Unilever sold its stake generating a 17x multiple on its investment. In addition, it transformed Unilever's own in-house approach and methodology in using and applying consumer research.

Intel does all this and more on a truly developed and global scale. It currently has a portfolio of nearly 300 different companies that it is investing in, some from start-up and some at later stage development. But it's not simply a way for Intel to work some of its free cash flow. All the investment opportunities are all born out of a guiding mission: how can Intel use its brand, its know-how, its assets, its partnerships to leverage further success in a digital technology landscape. So they invest in data centre software and cloud-based solutions, in the internet of things, in "wearable connectivity", in new software for manufacturing and tech labs, in new mobile data solutions, in different ways to process data using new tools and approaches…it's whole range of investment opportunities which gives Intel the chance to learn and to leverage.

On perhaps similar scale we can see a whole ecosystem of investment and innovation built up for example around Cambridge University. Around the university there are now 1,525 technology-based companies. They employ more than 50,000 people with combined revenues of around £12bn and market caps of approximately £50bn. It has led to this UK region having the lowest level of unemployment in the UK at just c. 2%. This venture capital focus has been going on for some 20 years and started with the University wanting to give its scientists and researchers the chance to grow and exploit commercial innovation outside the confines of the university itself. It has led to the Cambridge region being identified by the EU as one of the "top three innovation ecosystems globally" and has led to the development of internationally successful companies such as ARM, Autonomy, Chiroscience, Ionica, Solexa and many others.

Racing to do the same, we now see Google on its own extraordinary e-ventures investment spree. Research shows that Google has acquired more companies in recent times than any other organisation. They have made more than 120 deals in the past three years using their very substantial cash stock pile to purchase or invest in everything from new search processes to mobile technology to eg digital thermostat maker Nest labs for c, $3bn. "We want to use our skills to continue to develop Google for the future. That means exploring a whole range of different opportunities and not to stand still. We are fortunate that we do have the resources to make these investments but with technology changing so fast we owe it to ourselves and our shareholders to continue to innovate".

Many other companies are exploring ways to capture new technology opportunities. Amazon has set up 19 development centres across the globe and spends c. $2bn annually on R&D. It has also established a stand-alone new Tech company called A9 whose remit is to advance search and advertising technology for itself and to develop solutions to sell to others. Suning, one of China's largest retailers and revenues of $37bn, has set up for the first time a new investment /R&D unit overseas and has picked the US west coast as its location. Suning intends to invest in big data type solutions which will enable it to provide a more unified multi-channel integration for its customers. "This will ensure that Suning invests and partners for the future and find the best way to use new technology for that purpose". Walmart has set up @Walmart labs to find new ways to accelerate Walmart's e-commerce development. John Lewis, Rakuten (Japan's biggest etailer) and Tesco are among others who have also set up stand-alone digital and new tech investment and lab centres with a clear remit to innovate and develop new streams of revenue for the parent company.

★★★★★

It would seem then that a key way forward for many organisations is to establish something separate, a group of people with budget and resource to explore, innovate and develop new ways of operating and new ways of building and safeguarding revenue growth for the future.

It's about finding ways to learn, to explore new tech opportunities and to do so without being stopped by legacy ways of working. Companies are realising that if they do want to survive today's far-reaching technology revolution then they have to do this.

A key catalyst is the need to appoint someone like a Chief Digital Officer who can focus on these opportunities. Someone who is freed up from other business /day-to-day responsibilities who can focus on the future, who can champion digital technology, who can show the organisation what can be achieved by reference to best practices, lessons learned in the market place, introductions to new partners and experts. This sort of appointment is critical. Meaningful progress cannot be achieved by asking eg today's CIO or CMO to look at this area. They are already flat-out busy with the demands of the current business and making sure the company hits its quarterly /half-yearly metrics and targets. They haven't got the significant spare time to explore, investigate and truly innovate.

Companies like Intel and others have moved even further. Understanding the opportunity is more than just one about one hire or a couple of dedicated people they have gone on to allocate substantial funds and resources. But each company has to start somewhere, and if the senior team do accept the need and type of opportunity described here then it's key to examine the "how", the way in which this chance can be captured and realized and establish a dedicated approach to that.

Chapter 17

Digital Transformation
Key Lessons and Success Factors

A recent MIT /Cap Gemini study showed that 62% of all execs interviewed felt that "digital transformation" should be a top 3 agenda item over next 3 years. But only 18% felt that their organisations had really seized this opportunity.

For many companies, digital transformation has been mostly focussed externally. It's been about opening new channels to engage stakeholders and customers. It's been about setting up web sites, a mobile app, a Facebook page, a Twitter feed, perhaps some social media monitoring. Among B2C businesses there has also been a surge of development around e-commerce, finding new sources of revenue and growth.

These market-facing initiatives have often been successful. Large scale incumbents have begun to find their "digital feet" and are now major players in online commerce and customer engagement. The likes of Dell, Experian, Bank of America, Procter & Gamble, Macys, Next, Starbucks, Burberry, Bradesco Bank, Direct Asia and many other consumer-facing businesses have adapted and responded to market pressures and competitive demands.

But, still surprisingly few companies, whether B2C or B2B, have implemented meaningful programmes that look at how digital technology could also transform *internally* and impact *"the way they work"*.

There is in fact plenty of talk about this, conferences and seminars abound on the role of new technology solutions to transform a company. But that talk has *not yet* translated into many wide-scale corporate transformations. And this is being reflected in surveys like the MIT /Cap Gemini one. Most see the opportunity but few have yet truly grasped it.

Customer-facing web sites and initiatives are all good, and can clearly make a significant impact. They are also newsworthy and gain PR and shareholder interest. But many feel that the real digital opportunity lies more fundamentally in how the company is organised, the technologies it deploys, is it taking advantage of developments in the Cloud and Open Source, how it can evolve to be more streamlined and cost-efficient, automate processes, move to self-serve, how it can take advantage of technology to find new ways of working that ultimately lead to more and longer term advantages in its markets.

Let's look at some examples; here are some organisations who are leaders in this digital transformation field:

i. *Burberry:* Burberry truly began its investment in digital many years back. From early Web 1.0 days, it took the obvious key steps around relaunching its web site. It also took some fundamental decisions and adopted some key "digital technology" principles. First of these was to establish a common platform. They could see limited value in allowing each country manager to build their own web operation. One platform, one approach, one global governance to manage and administer that. These guiding principles have really helped ensure that Burberry could move forward with digital technology in a fast, coherent and coordinated way, cutting out duplication and allowing a truly global presence to develop.

    This way of doing business, this principle of how best to adopt technology innovation, then began to infiltrate inside the way the company operated, impacted its internal processes and ways of working. For example, product design became a fully digital process. Designs could be "shipped" digitally to suppliers and partners. People from all over the global Burberry community could input, share ideas, get engaged. Manufacturers had to comply and adapt to the Burberry way of working. Product development was not only more universal but the whole product cycle development time was substantially reduced.

    Burberry have been on a digital journey that has now lasted more than a decade. And it is still ongoing. The company is learning all the time what can be achieved, what typical roadblocks and obstacles it will likely encounter and how to move and adapt quickly. It has learnt that digital transformation cannot be viewed as one big change programme. The trick, the key lesson, is to look at this process by process. The goal is to identify a key process which could be improved by adopting a digital technology solution. Whether in product design, or in procurement, or in HR or in Finance, or in customer ordering or in in-store payment processing. Pick a process, pick an internal hero to champion the change.

    Among other things Burberry also has established its own "Innovation Unit". This is an internal team whose task is to identify the next key process to undergo digital transformation and then prepare the groundswell of interest, support and identify the enabling technology which can drive the change and deliver the target benefits.

ii. *Nestlé:* Nestlé made its decision to get serious about digital technology following a PR disaster in its use of social media and Facebook particularly. Nestlé CEO Paul Bulcke made the key decision that digital is now mission critical for the company and "key to get it right!"

This led to a series of reviews and a new digital investment strategy developed. Among other things there was recognition that a lot could be learnt from the best digital players. There was an opportunity not just to learn from best practice but also to leapfrog competition. So links were established with the likes of Amazon, Google and Facebook and people sent out on fact-finding missions to learn how to take full advantage of developments in digital technology. A dedicated Silicon Valley team was set up to get close to these leading edge organisations and learn how to "co-innovate".

In addition a "digital acceleration" team was set up at Nestlé HQ. Employees apply for a 6 to 12 month secondment for intensive training, to establish common understanding and ways of working, to bring that back out to local markets to enable faster coordination and adoption. There are now even "satellite training centres" in China, Italy and other locations. The overall goal is to establish new common shared global platforms, the ability to collaborate easily and efficiently, achieve the full benefits of scale from a global brand in its manufacturing, distribution and marketing, to implement new ways of working that incorporate digital technologies that can "permeate" the entire company.

One of Nestlé's key co-innovation partners has been Salesforce.com. While most companies will basically just buy the SFDC licence, Nestlé decided to establish with them a joint digital transformation leadership team. They established something closer to a business partnership rather than a vendor-customer relationship. There are joint teams, shared learning and know-how, the opportunity to develop together new IP and approaches which would be shared and a real commitment from Salesforce.com to see Nestlé emerge as one of its key customers and trophy case studies.

At the heart is the SFDC cloud /SaaS business model. But alongside that is a deep commitment to establish a single data platform that will give Nestlé a single global view of its B2B and potentially also its B2C customer data and enable insight that could drive better end-customer engagement, find new sources to sell-in the full product portfolio and new ways to generate revenue growth. The interest in getting this universal data view, to understand it and have the analytics capability to take advantage of it is seen as the key benefit.

iii. *Hays:* Hays is a global recruitment company and CEO Alistair Cox has been a consistent and vigorous advocate of the value of Digital and was an early implementer of a full scale technology transformation programme. The goal was to utilise new advances in technology tools to establish a flexible, scalable and adaptable platform.

The idea of hiring a major IT consulting firm like an Accenture or Deloitte or Cap Gemini to conduct a 3 year IT review and implementation programme with hundreds of external consultants at vast expense was seen as an outdated and inappropriate way forward.

The principle, in contrast, was that things are moving so fast, that any IT investment needs to be flexible and responsive to change, quick and easy to implement and able to be replaced without major risk or substantial new cost requirements. "If we're going to be successful in the future then we need to have an infrastructure that allows us to plug things in. And we won't know now what all those future "plug-ins" will look like".

Hays set about replacing its entire IT stack with support from open standards being a key priority in software selection. And for example, Cloud-based solutions would also be encouraged.

Hays set up a process review team. Its task was to do a process map across each of the key steps in the company's value chain. The aim was to develop a roadmap that identified which process would be tackled when. The initial goal was to find one or two major processes that had immediate support for change and which could make a big impact. Those processes which were more complex or where the benefit of change was uncertain, those would be put in a stage 2 or stage 3 group. They could be tackled better at later stages of the company's digital transformation journey, for when the organisation had more learning, know-how and confidence on how to go about implementing and easily capturing the change benefits.

Hays chose key software tools according to these guiding principles. They chose "posting vacancies on job boards" as a key process. And they wanted to have that process simplified, totally automated to enable job board posting, search and selection in a totally automated manner for both employers and prospective employees. "Search is the heart of what we do, it's our core process and critical we could get that right and continue to adapt it as technology evolved". For this solution, Hays chose an Oracle Intelligence Enterprise solution as its data warehouse for reporting and analytics, an infrastructure deploying PeopleSoft, a recruitment software tool from Bond Adapt and a Google Search application. All this was built with a tailored user-interface enabling Hays people to conduct the searches they would find helpful. And each of these solutions, especially from Bond and of course from Google came with an open web standards approach. The whole platform was completely web-enabled so all information could be shared and easily distributed.

"Now we can focus on the user experience and we don't have to worry about the plumbing and infrastructure, that is all in place. Digital leadership in this company has been a joint exercise involving all functions and departments. It's been an especially strong collaboration between IT and Marketing. We have done all this digital change to gain one advantage: that is our ability to engage customers and get more growth. And we 've achieved that".

Overview of lessons learnt/ keys to success

There is now a still relatively small but growing list of companies who have made real progress with their digital transformation. From global multinationals like 3M, GE and Cisco to smaller niche market operators like Farrow & Ball paints, IC International yarns and threads, Norgren fluid controls manufacturing, Bobcat Doosan construction equipment, Eden Springs water coolers, Pitney Bowes printer /office supplies…

Importantly these companies are shaping or reshaping themselves to make sure they are winners and still winning by the end of this decade. They have made decisions to stop talking about the need for change and the potential for change, but are now taking the tougher steps of working out how to get there. It's getting started on this migration journey that's key, with a commitment to it, an investment plan to back it up and a vision of the end-game and benefits, the size of the prize!

There are a number of key lessons about how to best go about this:

i. *Find an internal champion:* key is to have someone like a Chief Digital Officer, someone who can be the internal champion of digital change.

It's important that this person is not simply from a market-facing eg e-commerce background.
- They need to be able to understand technology deeply.
- They also need to be able to understand key business processes and perhaps have some knowledge of process "re-engineering".
- Commercial savvy
- Outstanding cross-company relationship-building/stakeholder management skills
- They need to be well up-to-speed with new technology and innovation

As it can be hard to find this combination of skills in one person, and given the scale and complexity that can accompany this change agenda, then some organisations are setting up a small central team that in combination has these skills and can work collaboratively to set the agenda and the priorities. That team might consist of the Chief Digital Officer, plus:
- Head of Programme Management
- Head of Technology Innovation
- People /Process /Culture officer

ii. *Define the size of the prize!*

Right now today there may be no "burning platforms", the business may be moving forward and while growth may be slow, profits are holding up. In which case the inertia factor will kick in/ the "why-change" when things are going ok?

Of course this digital transformation opportunity is not intended as any short term fix or boost to this fiscal's numbers. It is much more about the long term, about being in a position to win in 3 or 5 year's time, about working now to secure the long term survival and success of the company. It's the inertia factor of course which did for the likes of Kodak and which has killed off traditional bricks n' clicks retailers from Circuit City to HMV. It's not that these companies and others did not anticipate the upcoming digital challenges, it's just that they kept plugging way with existing business and operating plans assuming that the impact would be much later and they would have more time.

If there is one lesson in this fast-moving technology age, it is that things will happen more quickly than forecast, not less! As one IT exec has put it: "this company has spent the past 25 years building its IT and processes, it's now got about 3 years to reinvent them or we just won't survive. It's not just about changing some of the technology; it's about changing the way we do business"

To help address and manage these issues, it's important that whoever is championing the digital transformation agenda, gets to define what is the size of the prize, what are the key benefits, what might be the longer term customer and growth prospects, what might be the RoI potential to justify the business case, why do it. Some organisations in response to this challenge are establishing a key metrics and dashboard, a way of tracking progress toward an end-game where significant benefits are realised.

iii. *Integrated platform:* One key lesson that both Cisco and 3M have found is the need to build a single integrated data platform. Their aim is to build a common one stop view of all their customer activity. And ideally the aim is to make this seamless so that any function and department, whether Procurement, Finance or Sales can all access, contribute to and leverage that single unified customer history and record, no matter what the customer touchpoint, whether through call centre, sales team or direct and remotely online, or a combination of all. The benefit is not just a more impactful way of engaging with customers but it also can provide the customer with that single view of the company. So no matter what way they interact they will find common product, pricing, promotion and a real time updated understanding of their needs.

Retailers have been especially proactive in pushing down this path. To date, one retailer has stood out with the success it has achieved in this direction. And that is UK-based Aurora Fashion group. They own a number of well-known retail fashion brands and are now 6 years into their multi-channel single view of customer IT transformation. It works and has delivered constant and increasing improvement in margin, inventory management and most critically product line by product line, store by store revenue growth allied with a strong online sales effort.

Among other things, as their "digital champion" at the time Ish Patel has commented: "this approach has given us the data and the resulting analytical insight to better manage the business and maximise both sales and margin"

And another champion of this approach, Pfizer, has also commented on the value and importance of this approach: "Our top priority was to build a digital hub that created a common set of platforms and pipes. We were able to create real value from uniting the data from different platforms and silos and finding common insights across stakeholders to deliver greater value to them. What we didn't want as we embarked along our digital transformation journey was to have 1000 flowers blooming. They might all look nice but it just eventually leads to confusion. We wanted one version, one approach, one set of rules, one view of our customers"

Summary and Conclusion

This is such a big topic that it's impossible to cover all the ground here. So for the moment let's end with a couple of short summary points:

i.   A brief overview and summary from Axa Insurance:

"At Axa it was a learning curve for all of us. We had to start somewhere and be prepared to make mistakes. But we began with a core process that involved parts of our business and our customers, that was claims handling. We set up blogs and surveys to test out ideas and alternative ways of working. We opened that dialog set to employees and selected customers. We set up workshops with external IT suppliers to see if they could help us, and we picked suppliers who were lean mean and agile themselves, not the bigger cumbersome consultancies. We devised a new way of working with data in the Cloud, self-serve, streamlined procedures, real time data capture, fast response commitments. Once we decided what to do and what we wanted to get from this change, then we were able to launch a first phase in just 4 months. It surprised us. It completely changed our own expectations of what we could achieve. Now we feel we can change anything!"

ii. How to get things going, how to establish this major change culture around technology innovation:

Steering Committees are nothing new or innovative and many are not used well. But a key learning is that what works here is getting the whole organisation involved, not just one or two parts, pushing ahead with this transformation in integrated from, not in silos, developing some real momentum and not letting inertia creep in. Having this committee led, at least in the initial stages, by the CEO, involving colleagues from different geographies, departments and teams, managing the timetable, having full scale monthly reviews, setting clear targets and deliverables...all the well-known rules for success, but now making it happen in this demanding digital transformation context. That seems to be a key to success.

Chapter 18

Digital Transformation 2020

Key Case Studies

Digital Transformation is one of today's hot topics. Most every organisation and business leader will talk about it. This, from David Jones, when CEO of global advertising agency Havas is typical:

> *"Digital is our way to go. In today's world, you need to have global ambitions, but there is a size and scale where rapid change becomes very difficult. My single biggest focus is digitising our business globally. We need to develop a culture and capability where we can adapt and move quickly. We will need to radically simplify our structure. That is number one because it is very easy to slow down if we stay traditional"*

The big challenge that every exec now faces is to convert the well-received rhetoric into meaningful change and action. A recent study by MIT identifies what it calls a "digital imperative": *put digital first*, adopt *and embrace* new technologies and new ways of working or, they conclude, face competitive obsolescence.

MIT conducted a world-wide survey and found some surprising findings:

- 63% of business people interviewed said the pace of technology change in their organisation was slow, it "just lacked any sense of urgency"
- 62% said that digital transformation was just not high enough on the CEO's agenda: "we keep talking about it, attending conferences, setting up internal teams, but it all comes back to change and investment and we keep being told there are other priorities"
- 68% said that where there is digital change then it was mostly focussed on external customer-facing initiatives around web sites and mobile apps and not enough around internal opportunities to improve efficiencies, to streamline, automate and speed up processes and ways of working.

In the last chapter, we looked at 3 specific case study examples of how some organisations had already begun to deliver major achievements on their "DT" journey.

We looked at Burberry, Nestlé and Hays. It was clear that each had made a substantial commitment to digital technology-led change. Each saw itself as on a journey; a journey that would take not months but many years. In fact, "a journey that may never end!"

And because we live in a world where technology is right now evolving rapidly and continuously, then many execs now feel that in practice this journey might last for a good 10 more years. What was clear to people in the MIT survey, was that they could not afford to ignore this "digital imperative". If they did want to succeed then the CEO and the senior team had to mobilise and galvanise the *whole organisation*. It had to start from the top, it had to be widely communicated and explained, it had to be incorporated into *everyone's KPI*. It had to become part of the "way of doing business".

Here are some great examples of companies that are taking DT to heart.

John Lewis: as everyone based in the UK will know, JL is one of the most successful UK corporations. A retail group that dominates consumer shopping in grocery, apparel and homeware, has delivered consistent year on year growth across all its key financial metrics and now sees revenues at close to $15bn and continued upward trends in margin and like-for-like sales. Their CIO Paul Coby has been leading this technology-led change.

Like many, he sees the role of the CIO as fundamentally more challenging. "New technology is coming at us on all sides". But Paul has led JL in a continuous wave of improvement and change. Over the past 5 years, great progress has been made in building online capabilities for customers. Customers now can experience a joined-up multi-channel environment which connects store to online to mobile to social media touchpoints and provides an integrated experience.

That will continue. "But we are now getting deep into optimising our back end too".

JL recognise that if they are to deliver constant continual innovation in how customers can do business easily, smartly, conveniently then all the order-processing, logistics, fulfilment, invoice payment systems and solutions need to match up. And it needs to work all the way through the supply chain involving buying and procurement teams and key supply partners. Third party partners need to be as signed up to digital transformation as JL are and need to be able to participate in the JL programme as well as being committed to adapting and changing themselves.

"Our goal now is to modernise our back end. That is the big challenge. Many retail groups and other companies will have systems that are maybe 20 years old. That is stopping the organisation from adapting and moving quickly. We are now in the process of *ripping out* 50 or 60 legacy systems as comprehensive redevelopment. We are building a new technology infrastructure. We are fundamentally engaged in architecting and engineering what an omni-channel business will look like"

Developing the capability to do this is not easy. Just to keep pace with technology and how it is evolving is challenging. It requires continuous knowledge-building about the opportunities, continued assessment of new tech tools and developments. It requires a detailed understanding of best practices and lessons learnt. Understanding what new tech can bring, what parts of the Cloud, Open Standards, mobile connectivity for example are relevant and provide advantage. Not every new tech of course is right or is appropriate.

For John Lewis to have reached the point where it has identified "the 50 or 60 legacy systems to be ripped out" then they will have necessarily gone through a radical and thorough review, developed the business case and justification, all cross-functional and business heads will need to have been consulted and engaged, the risks, the time frames, the RoI will all need to have been evaluated, reviewed and agreed. They will have defined roadmaps, priorities, skills, who to lead which work streams, what capabilities needed, what milestones and specific targets to set for each quarter, each half year, each year end which will cumulatively add up to the stated vision.

To enable such an exercise many in the past would have automatically turned to one of the big consultancy groups, an Accenture, a Cap Gemini, an IBM or others. They would have signed up to a 3-5 year programme of change with scores, even hundreds of consultants crawling over the company, costing substantial sums. And if history is anything to go by then many such big tech programmes will have disappointed, coming in over-budget, over time and under performance. (I always recall one of the Heads of UK Government Procurement addressing a conference of senior IT execs and announcing that 85% of all government IT projects over the past 10 years had failed to deliver as promised! He was castigating and provocative, demanding explanations and improvement!).

UniCredit: one of Europe's largest retail banking groups, with €6bn of operating income, headquartered in Milan and operating widely across 20 countries mainly in southern and eastern Europe. UniCredit suffered like many banks in the credit crunch downturn, but has emerged as one of the new winning financial institutions. In a recent McKinsey interview, their CEO, Paolo Cederle, discussed the digital transformation journey that he has initiated and led across the Bank over the past 4 years. He calls it their Business Integrated Solution and it's still very much an ongoing programme. The objective was to redesign the IT environment so it could provide seamless, integrated front and back office solutions that took advantage of new enabling technologies and would set the Bank up to be a "winner in 2020".

Most importantly, UniCredit recognised the need to develop a culture of "digital innovation" throughout the organisation: "innovation is core to us, it's about the continuous improvement of services to our customers and to develop a new way of banking that is smart and cost effective. The market demands it and our customers and shareholders expect it. We have a commitment to invest in the development of leading edge solutions. New technology will be our key enabler. Our goal is to specifically link our internal functions of Research, Technology, Product Development and Marketing to provide new products and services that will drive our growth and our profitability".

As an example, UniCredit is establishing a new central shared services environment, targeting reductions in cost, quicker times to bring new products to market, improved working practices, better working environment to enhance internal employee satisfaction and productivity and design a more compelling and lasting customer engagement and experience.

UniCredit has also set up separate stand-alone teams or "factories" as they call it who are dedicated to eg new product development, or groups focussed on just one key process such as credit card processing with the objective of designing and launching a new solution in that space.

They have articulated a 6 step mantra:

innovation > flexibility > agility > transparency > time to market > cost efficiency.

"We are all about improving our flexibility and agility in how we work, be innovative in developing new quicker, more automated ways of working, speed up time to market and time to process customer interactions. This requires constant and close collaboration across the whole company, IT, Operations and Commercial. We can no longer afford to work in silos"

And in all this the role, structure and responsibility of IT is changing too. "IT staff still need and use their IT skills but they are not necessarily any longer a part of an IT organisation. The traditional org chart has had to be thrown away. Key IT managers are now often assigned to core projects and teams and may eg report to the Head of a Business Line. In our new credit card project we brought together Procurement, IT, Application development, Commercial, Compliance, Fraud Management and Customer Support into one integrated dedicated project group who all reported together to the Commercial Dir. It was disruptive change. But we have learnt that if we really want to win with digital transformation then this is what we need to do".

UNICEF: this is the world's leading charity working for children in some of most impoverished countries, but that has not stopped them establishing a "Digital First" programme of technology-led change.

Laila Takeh is a high profile Head of Digital for UNICEF. Her remit was to lead the organisation's digital transformation with responsibility to work across teams and departments to establish more effective ways of collaborating and working. "We recognised we need to become organisationally joined-up and could see how new digital technology tools could help us do that". They identified immediate improvements in ways to share data in real time, to collaborate more easily on projects no matter that key team members were in different parts of the world, join in key partners and stakeholders more seamlessly into various fundraising projects and initiatives.

"We needed to educate ourselves and learn and develop a broad understanding of technology as a group so that we could jointly design and improve how we did things. In a cross-organisation" environment we needed to develop the communication tools and processes at all levels to enable us to do this".

Laila has initiated several key things:

- "a digital hub", a group at the centre under her leadership who are champions of digital expertise, new technology options and this "digital first" change programme.
- an emphasis on better ways to communicate among internal teams using digital collaboration tools like Basecamp, Google Docs, wikis and internal social platforms like Yammer
- dedicate resource to staying up-to-date on technology and change improvement options

- develop a shared vision of how everyone would like the organisation to be; then work back to today and develop a roadmap of how to get there, how to reach that vision. "it may take years but we need to start somewhere"
- pick small steps first, "we decided to make a series of little bets"
- establish a culture where it's ok to make mistakes, "we can learn from our failures as well as our mistakes. From small wins and little failures we will find unexpected strategies and tactics that lead to big and extraordinary impact"

"if we had to sum up, our "digital first" is all about the appropriate use of digital technology to enhance the experience, increase engagement [and funding] and reduce overhead."

Barclays and Sainsbury's: Both these companies provide a good example of an alternative approach to digital transformation.

While they have both embarked on their own internal digital transformation programmes, they have recognised that delivering change and improvement will inevitably take time. Like John Lewis, they are having to identify the 50 or 60 + core legacy processes and systems that need to be "ripped out". And the change time required to do that is considerable while still managing risk and delivering uninterrupted continuity to customer service and the organisation generally.

That internal programme needs to happen. But are there other ways to take advantage of this digital world and use new technology advances to build new capabilities and solutions?

The model for Barclays and Sainsbury's is to establish a separate stand-alone joint ventures unit. They have set up a dedicated team with its own space, place, culture and the freedom to build and establish its own technology platform. They have looked to create something which is as close to a "dot com" style entrepreneurial unit as possible. Fully backed, invested in but without the encumbrance of large international matrix organisation system and procedure checks and reviews, without the hierarchy of numerous sign-offs and approval stages, without a bureaucracy that would otherwise stifle creativity and innovation. They have the freedom to move quickly, flexibly and with agility, hire people with appropriate digital skills and entrepreneurial attitudes, pay market rates for the right people, use Open Standard software rather than eg Microsoft dot net, partner with Cloud providers rather than trying to justify doing it all in-house, deliver new products to markets in weeks rather than years, and do so at potentially a fraction of the cost.

The idea at one level is just to recognise that there are now new ways of doing business, of building a company, that trying to do that inside a large organisation is difficult and so why not set up NewCo and give it its head? Other companies are also looking at similar initiatives and ask the question: if we were setting up this company today then how would we do it? For sure we would not build the same technology and process that we have today, it would likely be very different, so why not try that, see what it looks like? It may become our future. It may show us how to do things and NewCo may become the vehicle for how we do business. We may even end up migrating all our customers onto the NewCo platform, replacing and winding-down our existing legacy environment.

★★★★★

These case examples illustrate just how fundamental a world of change we are living through and just how deep companies need to go to take advantage of the digital transformation opportunity.

A recent McKinsey study tried to answer the question: is this change worthwhile, can it deliver a strong RoI, it's one of the most challenging change agendas a company can face, so given all the restructuring required, is it likely to pay back?

On average McKinsey found that "digital transformation can boost the bottom line by more than 50% over the next 5 years for companies that pull all the key digital technology and change levers. This is driven especially by building new ways to engage with customers but also about shifting customer interactions to digital self-serve channels and automating resource or paper-heavy processes…digital is providing the opportunity to reshape the economics of competition across all key sectors".

This study, as well as one from MIT, have identified 7 core basic steps that a company needs to take before embarking on digital transformation:

1. *Estimate the value at stake.* It will vary by sector and by market, but what is the potential size of the prize? To do this, estimates can be made on the size of the digital sales potential and the cost reduction opportunities available. These two strands -sales and cost- may need to be considered independently. While sales revenues may come from market-placed activity, web and mobile engagement, those sort of initiatives by themselves will not necessarily lead to a lower cost to serve. That needs to be thought about

as a separate opportunity in its own right. In the same way that John Lewis have a front end and separate though of course complimentary back-end programme.

2. *Prioritise*: no organisation can do this all at once; pick some early wins that look easier to achieve, the "little bets".

3. *Be ready to make some mistakes:* as UNICEF point out that might be the only way to learn how best to do things and what to avoid.

4. *Secure C-Level sponsorship and active support.* Research generally shows that still the majority of execs say digital change is too slow and suffers from lack of senior involvement.

5. *Establish a Chief Digital Officer:* this is someone who can be the champion of change. This person is the necessary expert on best practices, on what new tech tools need to be seriously evaluated and considered, what's out there in the Cloud that can be trusted and might accelerate things. This person ideally sits at the senior exec /Board table, asks the difficult questions about where are we on now on the DT change programme, is the voice of digital activation and opportunity, establishes the key metrics and milestones, reports on progress, evaluates competitor and other initiatives and makes sure digital learning is proactively shared and embraced.

    It's not an easy role, to be the voice of change and challenge and disruption. Vanguard companies in this space have learnt too that it can't be a lonely role. No good having it stuck in the back office with one person occasionally wheeled out to satisfy demanding shareholders. Much better to be a small but deliberately high profile team. Based at the centre and with counterparts in all the key business lines and geographies and departments. A virtual perhaps but unified group with a shared mission and purpose which starts from the top of the organisation.

6. *Education and learning:* to be successful companies need to cascade digital know-how and best practices throughout the organisation. It is as relevant to the most junior assistant as it is to the most senior team leader. This is where HR can step in to provide that means to learn. It may be through simple internal social networks or more formal e-Learning programmes, it may be through softer culture development or through establishing new individual performance measures and incentives, but it's essential to build up the drive for digital change and recognition of its potential bottom-up through the company.

7. *Identify key skill gaps:* This is a brave new world, it requires a readiness to change, a desire to learn new ways of working, a willingness and aptitude

for embracing technology and becoming technically literate, a confidence that in abandoning traditional ways of working that new more effective and ultimately more satisfying solutions will be found.

Not everyone is up for that. And as DT takes hold so it might be necessary to reskill or reorganise and restructure. One skill set that companies often lack is Programme Managers with the required skills and experience. Success or failure will likely hinge on just how good a Programme Director or Manager is in leading the defined change work stream. That person needs core project management skills and disciplines, but also needs to be at minimum technically proficient and at best technically strong so they can engage and interact with confidence and with authority with the IT team. They also need to have exceptional senior stakeholder management skills to get continuous support for the cross-functional, cross-country changes that are needed. And ideally all this in a digital learning environment and ideally with a relevant track record of success!

Such people do exist! But are not easy to find. Companies need to evaluate the benefit of having such people, the value they can bring and what is the right level of pay and compensation that will attract and reward.

★★★★★

Digital transformation is set to be the major catalyst for change till the end of this decade. A number of companies are now starting to set a 2020 vision and target, recognising that DT will represent their major opportunity for profitable growth over coming years. There's enough research and learning that shows this way forward is no longer an option, it's become a necessity, a "digital imperative" for survival and success. Few organisations today would argue against this "imperative", but the immediate challenge now is about converting the ideas into realistic and achievable change programmes that do deliver that winning position 2020.

Chapter 19

How Should B2B Companies be Taking Advantage of "Digital"?

Can "digital" drive revenue growth for B2B? in past few years, it's B2C companies that have been pioneering e-commerce and online customer engagement. But there's now a growing number of B2B companies finding a lot of success and opportunity from a more assertive digital path.

And "digital" does not need to mean direct e-commerce sales. That is an option but there is a wealth of easy steps and initiatives that can be taken online and with mobile that can generate growth, without even having to offer that direct sales channel.

A key concern for B2B companies: will more direct customer dealing affect current supply relationships? How will our Sales teams react if they see the company also selling direct online? Do our end customers even want to connect and or buy direct online and bypass traditional channels?

The learning is that channel conflict *is* a concern but that it *is* manageable. And there are many examples now about how to do that. What's more, companies that go down this path are now regularly reporting incremental revenue growth of anything between 5 and 20%.

Companies from global multi-nationals like 3M, GE, Cisco and Reed Elsevier to smaller niche market operators like Farrow & Ball paints, IC International yarns and threads, Norgren fluid controls manufacturing, Bobcat Doosan construction equipment, Eden Springs water coolers, Pitney Bowes printer /office supplies…there is a growing list of B2B organisations, or companies with some B2B products /services, who are seeing success through moving more into "digital".

Here are some key facts:

1. 81% of Purchasing /Procurement Managers said they would choose a supplier that offers an online ordering option over an equal supplier who

does not. The reasons were: (i) do business at our convenience, (ii) save time, and (iii) easily monitor order status (Hybris survey).

2. B2B revenues transacted online, not through EDI, rose to close to £40bn in the UK and c. $300bn in the US. (that US figure is more than the $200bn recorded in the US for online B2C transactions). These figures are expected to double by 2020 (Forrester report).

3. 25% of B2B companies in a recent Oracle survey said they now sold direct using e-commerce

4. and 80% of companies in that survey said that they are now actively reviewing this opportunity, whether to launch or invest further,

5. Mobile has become a key catalyst with 68% of companies saying that this had changed the way distributors and customers wanted to connect and trade

6. B2B companies generally are acknowledging this growing potential of digital and generally predict that e-commerce will become 50% of total sales. A number are claiming average growth rates of up to 30% + (Forrester /JP Morgan report).

Some have described all this as "the consumerisation of B2B". The same B2B buyers /procurement managers have just moments before been eg on Amazon.com downloading books to their Kindle, streaming music or a movie, and using the immediate and simple "one-click" order process. These same procurement managers are personally connected up, use tablets, use smart phones, like the latest gadgets, have children constantly trying out new web sites and online ideas. All that sets expectations. That ease of access, ease of use, ease of purchasing becomes a way of behaving and operating. And it is fuelling demand from customers big and small who want the same business purchasing opportunities.

But at the same time as this "digital" pressure mounts, so the learning for companies is: don't rush into this. There is a clear templated approach that has now emerged that shows a roadmap, a path, a way to push ahead on this journey.

The key is that this is a series of steps and learnings. It's about how to get things moving, how to take advantage and the pitfalls to avoid. There are essentially 2 key stages:

1. **Pre-e-Commerce**: *using digital to engage and interact with customers*
2. **e-Commerce**: *establishing a digital and multi-channel sales capability enabling customers to buy how and when they want to.*

There's a great story from a recent Cisco Sales conference. The Sales team did its annual review and saw there was one new customer who had purchased nearly $100m of equipment, and it had all been done in automated manner online. There had been no call centre or Sales force contact. And so, naturally, the immediate reaction of the Sales team was right, let's get our key Sales guys down there, let's get connected. But the customer declined the Sales call. Said they were very happy thankyou and preferred the ease and convenience of the online self-serve order process. Don't worry they said, we'll email you if any issues do come up.

Let's have a look at **Stage 1: Pre- e-Commerce**. What steps can the company take to get more digitally connected with customers, to create interest in products and services, to differentiate from competitors, to make it easy for customers to engage and purchase even it's the actual buying process continues to be through "traditional" and established supply routes and channels.

There are 6 steps or specific opportunities and things that can be done. There is no prescribed order but here is a practical plan:

* SEO
* Key functional tools
* Data capture
* Generate leads for Sales team
* Account management /order tracking /customer portal
* Social media

Let's briefly consider each of these:

1. SEO: Search Engine optimisation.

This simply means that when existing or prospective customers are looking to find out latest news, products available, which suppliers to contact, then a search on Google or other search engine will rank your company and its products to the top of page one.

And this is so important because research shows that searchers only occasionally go beyond that first page. And it's an easy thing to test:

For example a global B2B multi-national was looking to boost its digital market presence. They operated in the threads and yarns. But type in "threads and yarns" in Google and they were nowhere to be seen. Many of their key competitors however did appear on the list. Alongside a number of new niche more agile, "digitally aware" rivals. Bottom line, this company was getting no leads or enquiries through its online presence. While a rival proclaimed in its annual results that "new investment in digital has added significantly to our growth prospects".

And this is not difficult or costly to fix. There are now many SEO consultancies and experts who can work to optimise a web site presence. (type in SEO agency and you'll get a highly competitive list of the best, on page 1!).

2. Key functional tools:

www.pitneybowes.com provides a whole suite of functions that enable customers to "self-serve". For example they can request a brochure, access detailed product specifications, contact the PB Technical centre by email or call to get technical advice, read case studies that show how PB customers have used new workflow solutions to cut costs, get a quote, ask for a Sales department call back…all things that can be done at the customer's convenience and accessible from any device, via desktop PC, tablet or mobile.

www.bt.com/selfserve is aimed at Business customers. Its target is to "empower and enable our customers to get the best from BT". As well as offering a range of functions, it offers an AutoConnect self-serve product that enables its own B2B customers to offer "self-serve" digital solutions.

3. Data Capture

This simply means that whoever visits your site, you would ideally like to get their contact details as they may be a future customer or an existing customer who might have some questions before placing their next order. So this is simply about collecting that contact information. Simple idea, surprising rarely done proactively, and when done, then often not very well.

But what data is needed? Just an email address is all. Just a simple email address. How many times have we clicked on "Contact us" pages and found instead a long form to fill in. Immediate reaction is negative and there is often no wish to spend time filling it in or giving all that information. For example, one global insurer offering home insurance had a 3 page initial contact us form. Among other things asking for make and technical description of the home central heating system. Needless to say very few people completed the form.

It's all about the "value exchange". I will spend time filling in forms, only if I will get some immediate value back. Make it easy to leave an email address and the number of potential follow-up opportunities will increase.

Some companies eg Microsoft, Samsung will pop up a window after 2 minutes on the site, or just when the visitor exits with a "Thank you for visiting" message and an invitation to leave email address for follow-up contact information. And today, with cookies and behavioural targeting it is possible to have tracked that visitor experience and send a more personalised and targeted follow-up email with product relevant information.

4. Generate leads for the Sales force

Tyco, ADT, Cisco, Xerox, Sony Business all have for a number of years used their online presence specifically as a lead generator. And their web sites are all geared to that one particular goal.

This can be critical because many companies try to get their web sites to do lots of things. From providing news, investor info, press releases, latest results, brand imagery, videos, meet the CEO, long lists of products and services. And all fighting for attention and space on a crowded homepage.

The better digital companies have all been through that. They are further on the journey. They have learnt about simplicity and single-mindedness. Surely what's key, especially in today's more challenging economic conditions is to find every opportunity to drive sales. So why not get the web site to work hard for that.

www.adt.com/commercial is a good example. www.sony-europe.com/pro now has a well-oiled engine to capture data leads and deliver same day follow-up. JSP Manufacturing www.jsp.co.uk has a strong multi-channel approach combining call centre and fast online response. They have won recognition and awards for their online innovation.

5. Account management /order tracking /customer portal

www.solutions.3M .co.uk has on its main navigation bar a key tab: Partners and Suppliers. This leads to a series of partner, supplier and customer-facing account management /relationship-building initiatives. There is B2B Portal which product lists the entire 3M range of >5 million order lines and enables all ordering to be done online. There is the 3M Order Centre which enables customers to check status of orders and invoices. There is the 3M Extranet which provides dedicated and personalised customer and supplier documentation and account information. In addition there are optional facilities such as automated change requests, FAQs and workforce solutions.

6. Social media

A recent PWC B2B survey showed that social media as a means for strengthening business customer relations had reached a "tipping point". 48% of companies in the survey said they either had already appointed or planned to appoint an in-house Head of Social Media. Companies like Dell, PayPal, UPS, HP and many others were all quoted in the survey as saying that their engagement with social media forums and discussions had "materially contributed to revenue gains".

Dell is a now well-known case study. They have tracked more than $50m of sales directly as a result of "social media listening". Dell proactively participates in consumer as well as business user and prospective customer forums whether on Facebook, Twitter, Wired, PC Guide, CNET or any number of a dozen other widely trawled discussion sites. Dell has dedicated in-house people who monitor and contribute, and deal with complaints. "We turn critics into advocates". Dell estimates there are 25,000 daily social media mentions around the globe that are relevant and could impact their revenue line, positively or negatively. So "active monitoring pays back".

American Express "Open Forum" for business, RS Components, HSBC, Virgin Group through their Pioneers forum for new and small /mid-sized businesses…are all finding that this has become a key source of customer and prospective customer interaction

★★★★★

In summary, the Stage 1 "pre-e-commerce" opportunity is especially already rich in opportunity. For those unsure about what digital can do for their business, then why not start there?

Many B2B companies are now hiring experts from the B2C world to apply their learning and experience into their own markets. The principles are the same even if the target customer is different. And this can all be done within existing supplier relationships. It's all about building the Brand in the digital age and making a mark. And many of these initiatives can be established easily and at relatively low cost.

Chapter 20

B2B Social Media

There is growing recognition that social media can play a key role in B2B marketing. According to an e-Consultancy report B2B social media has reached a tipping point as it gradually becomes a mainstream tool for customer engagement and business development.

* Cisco recently decided it would use only social media to announce and market the launch of a new router product. This gave the opportunity to establish a wide-scale and immediately interactive environment where customers could look at video content and demos, ask questions, see what other customers were saying, arrange for a sales call, read through specs, participate in web and podcasts and generally engage. It has been acclaimed as one of Cisco's most successful ever launches. In addition this generated three times as much press coverage as their previous comparable product launch
* Dell has been developing its B2B social media now for several years and has learnt many lessons on its journey of how best to make that investment pay back. It now adopts "social media principles" in the way it engages with all its customers and also all its employees. It uses SM not just to communicate new ideas and plans but also to listen and learn so it can anticipate. Among other things it has a policy of actively monitoring all online brand conversations and turning those with negative views into advocates. It invites those people to its offices and assembly plants. It goes out of the way to make sure it addresses concerns as they arise and is proactive, not reactive, Dell say that as a result of this they have achieved "significant incremental sales". "Our customers are more influenced by what other customers say than what we say. In the B2B world that connection is even more important"
* American Express has launched OPEN forum which is a place for SMEs to share comments and ideas about not just AMEX products but about all

manner of SME type issues and concerns from bank borrowing, securing investment, tax, NI and a host of other things. "it's our equivalent of MumsNet, it's a place where business people can see what are the hot topics of the day, share, learn and engage. We have found a significant increase in corporate customer business flowing directly from this channel"

* BT (British Telecom) has had some similar success with TradeSpace which now has c.350,000 members and provides a general business social networking forum and place and which BT will use to announce new products and initiatives.

* Microsoft, HP, PayPal, RICS, UPS, RS Components are examples of other companies who are all taking positive steps to make social media work for their business customers.

A recent PWC survey also confirms that we are now looking at one of those "tipping points" where more and more organisations in the B2B space are now trialling, investing in and learning about how to make social media work for them.

Why is this? What's making this become a more important agenda item and opportunity?

It's not just the growing swell of examples and anecdotes in this area; it's also because of other factors:

i.   Mobile devices are enabling so much more connectivity. Prospective customers will be tweeting about a new product launch at trade shows or sharing immediate comment and observation about their reactions in online forums and it's crucial that the product company can monitor those conversation threads. And of course it's possible to proactively connect with those conversing and invite them to your trade show stand or for a follow-up demo and call.

ii. Employees expect more and more to be able to work in an environment where they can interact and collaborate to solve problems and share ideas. Social Media is displacing the now "old-fashioned" Intranet.

iii. Business audiences generally and buyers are influenced by the same forces that influence retail customers. Expectations are changing.

iv. Those companies who are developing social media strategies are finding that it lifts their whole customer communication to much more engaging level. Instead of somewhat dry and functional brochures and specs there can now be live and continuous human interaction.

v.   Cost reduction: in this climate of budget and cost consciousness companies
     like Cisco found that not only did their SM product launch work better
     than traditional ways of doing things but it was much more cost effective.
     It was also much more measurable and possible to determine exactly which
     elements generated the most leads.

With this area beginning to attract more and more attention, what are companies
generally doing about it?

In its recent survey, PWC found that 48% of companies had appointed
someone with at least part time responsibility for this SM area. 20% had
appointed someone full time, 12% had set up a small team. Only 13% had no
dedicated resource at all.

When the survey looked more deeply within organisations to explore what
the workforce wanted, then 75% of people indicated they would like to see
more social media deployment and through their company. This was as much
about enabling and supporting peer to peer communications as it was about
giving other opportunities and ways to connect and interact with existing and
prospective customers.

What PWC and e-consultancy and other observers are also finding is that
"dabbling" in SM activity is counterproductive. They liken it to the early days
of companies going online when many were still unconvinced about the value
or need for an online presence. Companies who approached that situation
half-heartedly got minimal if no return. And worse still if not done well, then
it led to poor customer experience and a negative outcome. What Dell and
others have found is that a small but sensible level of resource can quickly pay
back. And the gains are not just short term in terms of more business leads and
potentially new revenues. The longer team gains of more vocal and considered
customer support, the stronger Brand engagement and identity can lead to still
further positives down the track.

Chapter 21

Imagine the World of the Future

We're getting ever closer to a world which was first showcased in the Tom Cruise film *Minority Report*, a Stephen Spielberg directed movie. Spielberg wanted to present a plausible future and is said to have consulted with a number of scientists and technologists to provide a more realistic and authentic future scenario. 15 experts convened at a now famous 3 day "think tank" session. These included architect Peter Calthorpe, Douglas Coupland, computer scientist Neil Gershenfeld, biomedical researcher Shaun Jones, computer scientist Jaron Lanier, and former Massachusetts Institute of Technology (MIT) architecture dean William J. Mitchell. So there was some real in-depth thought and input that was being captured.

What was so innovative and exciting about this movie and why did its "sci-fi realism" strike such a chord? It was simply because you could sense that the showcased technology was in reach. Even though the technology did not exist at that time, nevertheless people could see how likely it could be and could believe in this future world. What is extraordinary is that a lot of the ideas in the movie are now in fact fast becoming real.

The most powerful visual idea in the movie was the way in which Cruise interacted with computer-generated imagery. He was able to speak with the computer. He could eg bring up a 3D holographic display of various screen pages and images from a computer memory bank. He could interact with that imagery using voice commands or by touch. He could manipulate /search content by a gesture to zoom, extend, move to the "next page" with simple touch or a simple hand wave. It was as though he was interacting seamlessly and completely with 3D and holographic displays. There was no sense of there even being pages from a computer, it was just content and material which could be summoned moved and sorted. The way Cruise's manipulation of content and imagery was presented in the film was as if he were conducting an orchestra. But this was an orchestra of content, not just people. They called it the "spatial operating environment interface".

Source: Imdb.com and Ign.com

News and information sources from Wikipedia and elsewhere have noted the future technologies depicted in the film were prescient. The Guardian published a piece titled "Why *Minority Report* was spot on". And Fast Company examined seven crime fighting technologies in the film similar to ones now actually becoming available. National Radio published a podcast which also analyzed the film's accuracy in predicting future technologies. One of the big ideas in the film was said by Hewlett-Packard to have been a major motivator to conduct further research in voice and touch computing.

Technologies from the film now being realized include:

★ Multi-touch interfaces put out by Obscura, MIT, Intel, and Microsoft for their Xbox. A company representative, at the premiere of the Microsoft Surface, promised it "will feel like Minority Report". When Microsoft released the Kinect motion sensing camera add-on for their Xbox gaming console, the Kinect's technology allowed several programmers, including students at MIT, to create what they called "Minority Report inspired user interfaces".

★ Retina scanners, by a Manhattan company named Global Rainmakers Incorporated (GRI). The company is installing hundreds of the scanners in Bank of America locations and has a contract to install them on several United States Air Force bases.

*   Insect robots, similar to the film's spider robots, developed by the US Military. These insects will be capable of reconnoiter missions in dangerous areas not fit for soldiers, such as "occupied houses". They serve the same purpose in the film-According to the developer, BAE Systems, the "goal is to develop technologies that will give our soldiers another set of eyes and ears for use in urban environments and complex terrain; places where they cannot go or where it would be too dangerous."

*   Facial recognition advertising billboards, being developed by among others the Japanese company NEC. These billboards will theoretically be able to recognize passers-by via facial recognition, call them by name, and deliver customer specific advertisements. Thus far the billboards can recognize age and gender, and deliver demographically appropriate adverts, but cannot discern individuals. According to *The Daily Telegraph*, the billboards will "behave like those in…Minority Report…in which Cruise's character is confronted with digital signs that call out his name as he walks through a futuristic shopping mall. IBM is developing similar billboards which plan to deliver customized adverts to individuals who carry identity tags. Like NEC, the company feels they will not be obtrusive as their billboards will only advertise products which a customer is interested in. Advertisers are keen to embrace these type of billboards as they figure to reduce costs by lowering the number of adverts wasted on uninterested consumers.

*   Electronic paper, developments announced by Xerox, MIT, media conglomerate Hearst Corporation, and LG the electronics manufacturer. Xerox has been trying to develop something similar to e-paper since before the film was released. When the *Washington Post* asked the chief executive of MIT's spin-off handling their research when "the "*Minority Report*" newspaper" would be released, he said it's already in trial in the lab. Tech Watch's article, '*Minority Report*' e-newspaper on the way", noted that Hearst was "pushing large amounts of cash into" the technology. In discussing the LG announcement, Cnet commented that "if you thought electronic newspapers were the stuff of science fiction, you're quite right. They first featured in the film *Minority Report!*"

So all this starts to bring colour and life to our future world and one that is very much just around the corner. Much of Spielberg's vision is fast becoming reality. The old dinosaur days of "point and click" will soon become a distant memory. We are moving to "Touch and Talk" world and are beginning to see signs of a Cruise type/ Gesture interactive type world that can be described as "Command and Connect".

As if this is not enough, we also have developments around "brain-driven" computer control where implants in the brain can be used to order and control the computer screen.

We are at the early stages of controlling computers just by thinking. Thought control has had especial early application for people who are paralysed. An article in Nature magazine shows how someone paralysed from the neck down can nevertheless control a computer, play games, change channels on TV, and manipulate a robot just by thinking: "Think and Move!" This brain to machine connection is getting ever closer and has relied principally on implanting electrodes to respond to the electrical activity associated with certain movements. An alternative method being trialled places electrodes on the scalp and the computer learns to associate particular brain signals with intended actions. A recent CeBIT show saw the launch of the world's first patient-ready commercially available brain computer interface. And there are many companies experimenting with such devices. And the cap that sits on the scalp to capture the brain movement is becoming more user-friendly and easier to wear. It's assumed that eventually no cap will be needed and the computer will be controllable just by thoughts alone. In the same way that a computer can recognise voice, it can also be "taught", it's believed, to remotely scan and pick up the brain's electrical impulses. (The picture here is of the Emotiv wearable headset which starts to make useable what was once functional and ugly)

Source: Emotiv EPOC neuroheadset

In fact, according to latest announcements from Intel, "chips in the brain will control computers by 2020". Researchers at Intel have concluded that it will only be a matter of time before we see the end of the keyboard and the mouse and surf the Net using just our brain waves. The brain would be enhanced by

Intel-developed sensors that are implanted. Experiments are currently taking place with robots and there are already examples of manipulating a robot using the brain of a monkey! It may sound far-fetched but the Intel research and 2020 deadline is serious. And this leads us on inevitably and inexorably to one of the ultimate medium term goals of developing genuine artificial intelligence. There are today many research teams across the globe looking at how to integrate software to enhance the processing speed and power of the human brain and to potentially add new knowledge immediately via a plug 'n play routine!

Significant effort is currently being devoted to making human interaction with computers and with information in general more simple, natural and seamless. "The pace of advances in computing, communication, mobile, robotic and interactive technologies is accelerating dramatically", Ahmed Noor points out in a recent review in Mechanical Engineering. "The trend towards digital convergence of these technologies with information technology, virtual worlds, knowledge-based engineering and artificial intelligence is beginning to usher in a new era"

And Noor goes on to say: "there will be a dynamic aggregation in the future of humans, cognitive robots, virtual world (cloud-based 2.0) platforms and other digital components to create a new ecosystem. Humans will have multi-sensory, immersive 3-D experience and capability in a mixed physical and virtual world…the emphasis will be on optimising human performance"

The human experience of the computer to date has been for us to immerse ourselves in it, we have had to learn to work in the computer's world of scroll bars, list controls, mice and key board. But we don't live there. Even with the iPhone we are still interacting with the device on its terms in its world. But, we exist in our own three dimensional world. And what will start to happen is that the computer will increasingly come to us. It will start to recognise who is sitting in front of it or who is holding it. It will recognise our voice and react when we talk to it. Breakthroughs such as the Xbox Kinect and Gest-Cube show that the computer can learn to react to *our* physical movements and the advance in BCI (brain computer interaction) demonstrate further how we will be able to exert control, on our terms and in ways that suit us, not chained to the desktop!

Here's one vision of the future from Sam Martin speaking at a Forbes magazine conference about our world in 2020:

Source: Media@frogdesign

"In the future every visible thing will be catalogued and indexed, ready to be instantly identifiable and described to us. Want to go shopping? In the future we won't need big retail stores with aisles of objects on display. We'll be able to shop out in the virtual world. Do you like that new car you saw drive by? Or those cool shoes that person is wearing? All you'll have to do is look at it, and your mobile handset or AR (augmented reality) equipped eye-glasses will identify the object, look up the best price and retailer and with the voice command "buy it", it's yours!"

This future is all going to be about the way that humans can interact with computers. Digital technology will be everywhere, everything will be reducible to digital data, and will have been recorded and therefore become accessible. Instead of sitting in front of a PC or holding a tablet, computers will be built into everything around us and interaction will happen naturally. They will become "invisible tools which will blend into everyday life".

The next generation may never see a computer screen in the physical and formal way that has been used up till now. They will summon content and information on the go wherever and whenever they want it, they will organise and select from it in whichever way they want, they will send it to friends/colleagues by simple voice command or hand wave. As a result you won't even need to carry a mobile phone, you'll instead be able to access wifi or 4G or other networks and simply say a number or pick it off a called-up content sheet. News can be summoned and read via holographic display or on electronic paper and can be "dismissed" when no longer required. It will be an extraordinary new world and by 2020 we will already be seeing this sort of environment gaining critical mass.

Eras of Computing and Human Interaction	
1990 to 2009	*Point and Click*
▼	
2009 to 2012	*Touch 'n Go!*
▼	
2012 to 2015	*Touch 'n Talk*
▼	
2015 to 2018	*Command 'n Connect*
▼	
2018 to 2020	*Think Talk Move*

Chapter 22

A Few Big Companies Already Dominate!

It's clear that our future world of communications and business is being radically changed by digital technology and innovation. What's startling is that this is being master-minded by just a few multi-national organizations. They already are dominating and their influence is going to grow.

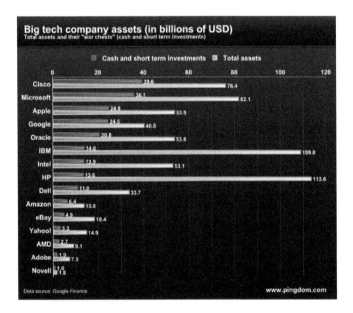

* Google own YouTube. They also own DoubleClick, AdMob and a host of other general and niche market-leading businesses. They have acquired more than 100 companies. They have invested in fields as diverse as robotics, gesture and facial recognition and wind turbines! They vigorously promote Google Chrome web browser as an alternative to Internet Explorer, Google Cloud, Android (the now global leading mobile phone operating system), Earth and Maps, Google TV, Google Glass and many other truly innovative applications. While much of their investment activity is focussed on start-

up ventures, they still managed to spend $12.5bn acquiring Motorola to provide more global access, $3.5bn on NestLabs to enter the home automation /consumer "internet of things" space and $1bn on Waze GPS software to tie everything into a location-based, personalised solution.

★ Microsoft has spent $4bn snapping up Nokia, buys Yammer (the leading enterprise social media network) for $1.2bn cash and $8.5bn of its cash reserves acquiring Skype, a substantial premium given Skype was at best break-even and certainly not making a profit. But it does give Microsoft access to a 663 million global community. It has a 1.6% share of Facebook and a small shareholding (albeit <5%) in Apple. It has acquired some 150 other companies or strategic stakes in the past 20 years and typically acquires around 12 companies each year!

Google, Microsoft and a few other dominant global tech companies together have huge cash war chests. Microsoft had some $35bn at time of writing, Apple had c. $25bn and Google had some $25bn. And other Tech companies like IBM, Cisco, Intel, HP and Amazon are all cash rich. In fact, the top 12 Tech companies listed in the US have a staggering $215bn of cash searching for investment opportunities. They are among the most valued on the planet.

These are the companies that are changing our lives. These are the ones that are leading the biggest revolution in history. These are the ones that are set to continue to lead the transformation of the global economy and the way human beings interact and communicate. Even as we read this book, history is being made.

Chapter 23

Digital Check-List for Making it Happen!

In this era of digital innovation and adventure, it is now much more challenging for a Brand to engage with its customers. In the "good old days", there were relatively few choices. There were three main channels of engagement and distribution:

- Above the line (ATL): meant a mix of TV (if the brand budget could afford it), typically some press/print and if feeling bold a radio ad.
- Below the line (BTL): leaflet /sample distribution to people's homes
- In-Store: point of sale incentives and information

A brand marketing team was used to that set of choices. Agencies were skilled at understanding those specific options and the work load could be divided between two or three agencies: one for the ATL, one for the BTL and one for other stuff! But now, as the twenty first century gathers pace, it's all become a lot more complicated. At the last count there were at least 30 different channel and communication options:

Multi-channel options

TV broadcast 30" or interactive, Cinema (3-D or not 3-D?), Radio, Print, Mobile ad or content sponsorship, apps for smart phones, apps for tablets like iPad, pod casts/vod casts, Bluetooth mobile, Direct Marketing, e-mail, catalogue, telemarketing, sales reps, poster, outdoor/event, kiosks, vending, PR, Social Media, Sponsorship, In-game advertising, Point of sale, In-store, on cart, website, online advertising, Search, viral video, affiliates…

It's become a bit of a dinner party game these days to see if you can identify any others! There is just a bewildering array of choice for any brand marketing team and an almost impossible set of decisions about channel mix, budget allocation, which channels to prioritise, which can be ignored. In addition, the audience that a Brand must reach has now become fragmented and widely dispersed and does not consume media in the easy-to-reach passive way that they used to.

TV, once the home of mass audience reach, is now fragmented and unreliable. It has soared from a few mainstream channels to many hundreds. It's available live or in catch up, via cable or satellite, via internet-connected TV or even down the broadband phone line. People no longer just watch right through a programme. They can skip through ad breaks eg on Sky + or Tivo. They multi-task and might have one eye on the TV set, another on their Facebook page and also be watching for tweets and emails on Twitter and/ or speaking with friends via Skype or instant messaging. Engaging with this audience in the most efficient and effective way has become mesmerising and complex:

- which channels deliver the best ROI?
- which campaigns work best on which channels?
- if we communicate via channel A then is there a "must-have" complementary channel B that also needs to be involved?
- is there an ideal channel mix?
- can we "afford" to ignore eg social media or mobile?
- or could we "afford" to ignore expensive TV and switch to apparently lower cost online?
- does the channel mix vary by season?
- is there a different channel mix for different target customer segments?
- given that it's all changing so fast and new channel opportunities are emerging, how can we check that what we plan for this year is going to be relevant and appropriate?

The start of an answer to these questions is to best understand what the target customer prefers. But such research can be time-consuming and expensive and would need to ideally cover all types of segments and audiences and like a lot of research may well be inconclusive. So how about an easy top-down approach?

6 step test: a brand check for the digital multi-channel age?

Here's a quick 6 step test to see how far your Brand has already travelled in moving away from traditional media channels and becoming more of a digital multi-channel brand. Each of these steps uses free tools and analysis. They are quick and easy to do.

1. *Go to Adwords.google.com/targeting*
   Type in the name of your brand and you will get an instant analysis of monthly traffic, global and local searches as well as any click through analysis if the brand is being advertised on Google already
2. *Go to Google.com/insights/search* and you can see the traffic analysis over time, last year, last week as well as related content/articles that might be influencing those search levels, you can also search at local, country or global level
3. *Now go to Alexa.com* and you can look up your web site and start to get comparative traffic data looking at your brand site versus others in your category. It shows how high the web site ranks in terms of traffic generation.

   And amazingly, there is a whole consumer demographic and segmentation analysis that tells you eg: by age, gender, education, family and location.

   It will also tell you where your web site traffic is coming from so you can work out eg if your Brand is say Pepsi, that the number 1 connecting site in UK is Sky Sports. That will tell you about existing campaign effectiveness, which ads working which not (eg the ads on Yahoo are not working). But will also start to give you a lot more info on the size and type of your online audience

   You can begin to start understanding whether and to what degree your Brand is participating in this digital world
4. *Next go to Facebook.com* and at the search facility type in your brand name. You will immediately find the number of Facebook fans and friends you have.

   Again you can type in competitor brands and see what their numbers are. Is your Brand being left behind in the social media race? Or is this whole category just not of sufficient interest for people to want to talk about it

   And even more helpfully, you can find out what people are saying about your brand, good and bad. And a similar exercise can be carried out on Twitter.com where the postings and tweets and number of followers can be very immediate and responsive to any marketing or advertising activity.
5. *Next, go to Technorati.com* where again for free you can use their Search facility which will review the "blogosphere" and find all recent and current blogs about your Brand or any related topic of interest.(www.twingly.com provides a similar search and functionality).

6. If you want *"a one search find all approach"*, then go to *www.socialmention.com* which will trawl through the Net "searching content from across the universe" as they say. They will look at all blogs, news, video, audio and images. You can sort by date and by source. It will tell you where comment is coming from and what are the "buzz words" that are generating that comment. But most helpfully, they will also give you a "Sentiment score".

- This will tell you number of mentions which are positive, negative or neutral.
- It will also give you an overall sentiment score (ratio of positive to negative comment).
- there's also a Strength of Sentiment score, which is the percentage likelihood of the brand being discussed in a social media environment
- there's a Passion score which is the percentage likelihood that people talking about your brand will do so repeatedly
- lastly there's a Reach score which is a range of influence metrics and identifies the number of unique authors referencing the brand divided by the total number of mentions. That will help check if it's a few people mentioning you a lot or many with just a casual interest.

This tool will even give a list of the internet names of the top users/people who talk about this brand and give you a link to them. It's a wonderful way of getting in touch with people who could be or could become key influencers, who may themselves have lots of friends on Facebook and followers on Twitter and themselves can set the tone and reaction to how a product is perceived and rated.

And all this is for free! And there are other analytic tools like this eg Filtrbox which is now owned by Jive Software. Here you can get a free trial but unlike Social Mention, they have understandably taken a more commercial approach where you are required to sign up for the free trial and they will then look to convert you into a customer paying for the daily/weekly or monthly "buzz monitoring". Their analysis is presented in a more graphical format so can look easily too at patterns over time and compare with key competitors. Radian6 (part of Saleforce.com) and Infegy. com provide a similar service.

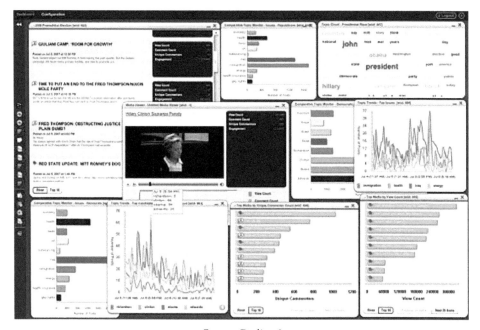

Source: Radian6

Yet another example, still for free, is Addictomatic. This site enables you to custom build and create your own web page with blocks of content regularly updated taken from eg Bing news feeds, Google blog search, Facebook, Twitter, YouTube and Instagram.

And there are any numbers of software companies and brand consultancies offering for a fee to look at these brand monitoring sites and provide a report of what is going on out there in the digital world, how digitally engaged is the brand audience, how responsive generally is your product market or sector to a multi-channel approach, are there any learnings from what competitors are up to and, without too much analysis, how important are social, mobile and the other multi-channels becoming for short and medium term sales and marketing planning.

Some Brands have assumed that they are just not relevant enough to generate much social comment, especially if they are B2B, thinking that any negatives in product or service would remain customer-specific, under the radar and manageable in the traditional way. But in this topical, instant, multi-channel, "news now" and global world, that view can be violently disturbed if something does goes wrong.

As Warren Buffet has said:" it takes 20 years to create a brand and twenty minutes to ruin it…if you think about it like that then you will certainly do things very differently!"

Chapter 24

Case Studies
Building a Successful Online Business – Lessons Learned

Three key questions drive this chapter:

1. What's required to build a growing, profitable and sustainable online business?
2. What marks out the winners?
3. What are the lessons learnt?

We can look at a number of outstanding case studies.

Case Study 1: TripAdvisor

TripAdvisor has become the leading global advice centre for holiday, hotel, flight, restaurant and general trip planning. It provides coverage of every major destination across the globe. It will check other travel intermediaries like Expedia, Opodo, Orbitz, eDreams and consolidate the information from every airline flying for eg the designated departure airport to any destination.

And the search engine is operating increasingly close to real time (though data updates vary depending on real time news feeds from each airline). The amount of data being crunched in each search is considerable and yet it's done in seconds. Its reviews, ratings, testimonials can make or break a supplier. Its search alerts can update on availability or relevant news, link in via Facebook so you and your pals could book online together and now uses GPS to provide up-to-the-minute local holiday search info. Its Book Now! service has become a leading booking engine. It now operates in 14 languages across 23 countries worldwide and covers 24,000 destinations attracting 40 million visitors each month.

The whole global reach, product and service multi-channel operation is immensely impressive. Its market cap is around $10bn.

And when was TripAdvisor first launched? Just in 2000. And launched at the time when in fact Web 1.0 was bust, when the internet bubble was bursting, when doomsayers were saying there's no future for businesses on the Internet, when naysayers, and there were many at that time, even if they could acknowledge the consumer convenience and benefits, would never invest anything significant.

What the founders of TripAdvisor have demonstrated is *how* you can build a substantial business on the Net. They aimed to become the "category killer". They wanted to be the destination brand that everyone went to. They asked how can we be that "first port of call"? They found backers in Flagship Ventures in Cambridge, Mass, in 2000 who were themselves passionate about online and believed in its long term potential. They gave the management team the time and the commitment to build a technically complex and demanding web site environment that could manage the huge number of real time data feeds and align that with a sophisticated search engine. What TripAdvisor does today has become more commonplace and easier to achieve but it does still take a lot of time, commitment and ingenuity to get there.

Payback came in 2005 with the sale to IDC who immediately put TripAdvisor together with Expedia. IDC continued to invest heavily putting in a further $350m to get the site to the global, multi-country scale it is today. The company IPO'd in 2012 and some commentators suggest that the current market cap undervalues the "social community" aspects and its continuing ability to attract millions of visitors, its brand name and its category-killing status.

Case Study 2: Amazon.

Why have they been so successful? There are 3 key reasons:

i.   first and foremost it's simple, single-minded idea and highly functional. Type in name of book, film, music etc and up comes a ranked list. The format and presentation has hardly changed since it first launched.

ii. it's very very easy to use. One click and you can buy. You can complete a transaction in seconds. I have often commented on this functionality. It is exactly what internet buyers are looking for. The general internet mantra is "quick, easy and convenient". If a site experience can past that test then it's got the core platform to succeed. Sounds straightforward, where's the complexity of that? But how many other sites offer a one-click functionality? They will ask you to log-in, remember your user name and password and often expect you to complete all the credit card details all over again. And even if you can get through that then you are often shunted off to some Visa verification site where you're expected to remember yet another password. But hang on, I've visited and bought from this site before, why can't they be like Amazon and just remember me?

The more clicks the visitor has to make to complete a purchase the more likely they will not complete and will abandon the shopping cart. Most abandon rates are typically between 40 and 80% which is already alarmingly high. How did you manage to lose a customer who had got that far into the process where they had liked what they saw, selected it, got ready to buy it and then 40 to 80% drop out! With Amazon one-click, you can see how that loss in minimised. One click and they've already bought! But research shows that more than 3 clicks and consumers start to get frustrated, after 6 clicks there are significantly diminishing returns and after 12 clicks, the rate of abandon quickly hits the 80% plus mark.

So why would anyone design a click-heavy site?

Extraordinarily, in this fast changing and competitive landscape, Amazon still stand out a mile in this respect. Not surprisingly they have seen off alternative online usurpers like Bookseller, Waterstones, Borders outside of the US, and Bertelsmann Bol.com, all of whom have flirted and tried to compete with Amazon's core book product line and failed to grab any significant market share.

"Easy to use" should be something every site now scores well on. But they don't. We can continue to see long lists of "worst web sites". Many especially B2B companies continue to put out "brochureware" with no purpose. Visitors can find pictures and sometimes even videos but if they'd like to contact someone at the company to make a purchase then there's no email address, no phone number, no names, just bland information. What's the point? How is a company going to get any RoI on its digital presence? What's the point? How much business /sales leads are they losing? Who is the site designer that put this together and thought this was a good idea? Who paid for it and why did they not ask the fairly simple and obvious questions? Why does this happen? Why do the obvious mistakes keep occurring?

iii. The third test is that the "page must load immediately" (and countless research reports from Forrester make this point). Why is this so important? According to Forrester:

- 57% of consumers will abandon a web site if the page does not load within 3 seconds
- estimates are that a company can lose c.50% of its potential online sales if its pages don't load quickly
- for every second of delay in page loading, the viewer will spend less time looking at the page once it does load and in particular will not absorb any secondary promotional content or links

Case Study 3: MyFaveShop.com

A couple of years ago, I observed at first hand a new e-commerce venture which became called MyFaveShop.com. The idea could be described as follows:

It was all about "social shopping". As you browsed the web you could click on anything you liked. It might be an item of clothing, an intended present, a Xmas list. Instead of that appearing in a long Favourites list, you could capture the image and the product detail and put that into your own specially designed shop. You could then invite friends to see your "collection", all laid out in a 3-D like retail store environment. And you could decorate and furnish that store in your own style. So you could say, put together a group of 4 or 5 dresses or coats you liked and had plans to buy one for the season. You could invite your friends to look at them and get their opinion on what would suit best. And then, if you wanted you could click and buy.

The core idea was "shopping together", co-browsing so you could look at the same screen together remotely in real time (eg ask sister Edith in Australia if she thinks this dress would suit Mum currently wintering in sunny Florida!)

But however nice the idea, it has taken a couple of paragraphs here to describe and illustrate. And therein lies its complexity. In contrast, Amazon takes one very short sentence to define: look at a list of products, select and buy. MyFaveShop however involved a lot of ideas and messages and because it was new and there was nothing like it at the time to benchmark or compare it required a lot of explanation to people visiting the site for the first time. How define in one short sentence what this was about?

So when this came to developing the simple, easy to use web site and navigation things got complicated. There was a whole variety of messages and explanations and illustrations all vying for prominence on the home page. Each member of the team had their own judgement on what should be the order and the priorities. The investors had their own marked preferences too. And even the consumer research that was conducted proved inconclusive. Some liked the idea, others didn't and each picked up on different aspects of the proposition:

- "I like the idea of social shopping"
- "design your own shop…that's cool"
- "put all my favourite things in one place"
- "create a wish list of things I want"
- "looking together at the same screen"
- "I like the choice of shop designs and being able to paint and furnish it how I like"

To complicate things further, it was clear that some visitors to the site would be web savvy and would "get" the concept quickly, need little hand-holding and want to get on with the site experience. While others would need more show and tell and so need an introduction and explanation. And finally, there had quite clearly to be an income stream so it was important that visitors got the message that they could browse and buy. At the same time there were key ad messages from brands that had to be found space and get incorporated!

The web team started to get very bogged down in the detail and trying to find the right web experience. Does the home page lead with the introductory explanation and even a step-by-step video or does it offer a navigation which tries to tempt all the different types of users and visitors. And what about repeat visitors? How get them engaged enough to register in the first instance? What type of data capture should be requested? At what stage in the visit is registration best requested?

The web site did launch, struggled out of Beta and was eventually and somewhat mercifully sold for a price, that at least gave some return, to another e-commerce organisation, who themselves found they were gradually forced to simplify things and in the end it became more and more like just another shopping web site.

It was a shame because there were some great ideas here and if the messaging challenge had been solved, if the right prioritisation had been found, if the user experience had been put together in a simple and easy to use form, if the investors had had more patience (or is that indulgence!), if the team had been able to cut through the complexity and for example found a way to start with just one big idea while adding other complementary messages and functions later, then this could, perhaps, have been a winning web site. But the learnings here from a disappointing experience can be just as compelling as ones about a successful one!

Simplicity is without doubt a virtue when it comes to designing web sites, content for mobile, Apple apps or any other stuff for a screen. That "home page" is a small piece of real estate, it's precious, the people who look at it are typically impatient and expect something quick, easy to digest, intuitive and arranged in such a way that they can very very easily make a decision to invest in this experience or click away. Most web sites have overall "fall-off rates" of over 90% from their home page. In other words most never make it to page 2. Why have Google and Facebook been so quick to catch on? While there may be many reasons, part of the explanation lies in their beautiful simplicity. You know immediately and unequivocally what they are all about.

Why is user experience simplicity so crucial? Research from Forrester and others highlights the following:

- they found that most people, if they could not immediately, within 3 seconds, understand what the site was about then they would leave.
- 8 out of 10 people will not revisit a site after a disappointing experience.
- in today's instantly networked social world, 35% of those who did have a disappointing experience say they will proactively tell friends not to visit that site.
- research from the Aberdeen Group shows that a 1 second delay in page load times equals 11% fewer page views, a 16% decrease in visitor satisfaction and a 7% loss in conversion. And as an example, Shopzilla improved average page load times from 6 seconds to 1.23 seconds and experienced a 25% increase in page views and a 12% increase in revenues.
- more than 60% of mobile users who visited brand web sites, found that mobile access was slow and information on the screen cluttered and sometimes unreadable.

4. Case Study: General Motors

In general, 58% of people research a product or service provider online before buying according to PC Mag. In the auto sector that % goes up to 82% according to AutoTrader. Buying a car is a complex decision-making process as buyers compare and contrast models, review specs, read brochures, look at video content showcasing the car and the driving experience, and that's well before they've visited the showroom. Further research has shown that the auto sector is unlike other high ticket value items. With say the buying of a new TV set, consumers will use online to narrow down to a couple of different brands eg the "Sony 4G" and the "Samsung 3D". With research into cars however, people will use online to decide which brand they are going to buy and they will prioritise one only eg I'm going to buy a Ford and then will have in mind a couple at most of different model options. So online is even more critical in the auto sector. Make the online experience compelling and you drive your prospective customer right to your selected brand dealer showroom.

What the research goes on to say is that almost noone (there are exceptions) will buy a car site unseen and without "kicking the tyres", but even though the brand web site doesn't "sell" anything, its influence is still just as "mission critical".

General Motors in the US were one of the first car manufacturers to really understand the value of online. Inspired by examples from digital agency Modem Media, GM created MyGm.com. It was a place for the GM enthusiast. Find out more about cars and get access to much more than you'd find on the basic web site. Register for news and invitations to special events and opportunities to drive the latest cars. It was also where the owner could register details of their own car, get reminders of services, get latest model upgrades and changes etc. It was one of the first very successful online loyalty-driving programmes which worked!

5. Case study: global law firm.

If there are no limits on B2C, then what about the B2B arena? It's been argued that services which are complex, like legal services, are just not appropriate for an online world. Many lawyers felt that if a client wanted to decide which law firm to choose, or get expert advice then that could only be done with face-to-face contact and building a personal relationship. In fact so arrogant were most law firms that they hardly bothered with a web site and many just put up a token piece of brochure ware. However, even law firms, no matter how high end and sophisticated have belatedly begun to realise that the online world might just, just, be a little more important!

Here's an example from a top 10 global law firm. They had seen profit pressures due to market competition. Some redundancies had been made but mostly to ensure and protect levels of partner profitability, which remained high. In this context, the firm had not developed its online presence beyond a fairly basic web site. But many in the law firm did not think that improving or investing in the site or more generally online would be worthwhile. How many people visit the web site and certainly how many would be influenced by it? Surely it was all about personal recommendations and personal networks, this online stuff had no relevance. And as for things like a strong presence on search engines or a social media strategy to engage with potential new staff trainees and associates from school, well, that was something for the likes of Coca-Cola, "not us".

However, a new marketing director had been hired who instinctively felt that the web had more influence and so some simple market research was conducted. Let's go talk to our target customers and actually ask them, direct, are they influenced by what they see online?

The answer that came back stunned the lawyers. After all they don't expect to get things wrong. But the research findings were absolutely based on what their new target clients were saying. The message back was loud and clear and more or less unanimous:

> *"for us, the web is the firm's window on the world…it's the first place we go to rather than look at brochures or fancy white papers…we expect a certain standard online, the kind of standard we'd expect from a top law firm…if we don't see that then we're going to start wondering if what we see online reflects the quality of the advice we'll get offline"*
>
> *"yes, in something so personal and complex as legal advice we'd usually want to meet the firm and people we're going to work with…but when we're deciding on the pitch list we will do our due diligence and we find that starts with the web site"*
>
> *"we don't mind slick, we don't mind a bit cheesy but we do expect class"*
>
> *"yes, if I visited a firm's site and did not get a good and positive impression then it would change my mind about using them"*

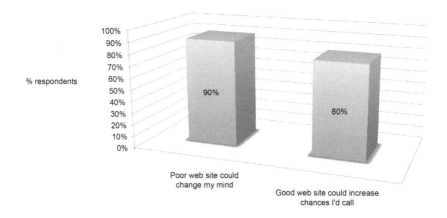

The firm's web site was appalling. The home page for example featured an interview which was nearly 2 years old with a partner who'd subsequently left the firm and a client who was so obscure they sounded like a small local doughnut company. Practice areas often had no content and it was sometimes hard to see if the firm had any expertise in its listed areas of activity. Worse still, how to contact the firm, who to contact and their phone number was hard to find. And when, eventually, it was possible to find an email address, it was a generic info@) address. That might have been ok as it promised next day response but the info@ inbox was rarely checked so genuine enquiries from prospective new clients most usually went unanswered!

And while the new staff/careers section was a bit more dynamic and up to date, it had little information and the key social web sites for aspiring lawyers like RollonFriday and LawCareers carried content from most of the rival firms but nothing from this one.

The list of site negatives went on and on and it was only when the senior partner group saw the hard evidence that they did finally agree, and still somewhat reluctantly, to invest in a site update and revitalised online presence. And here is a firm with a turnover of more than £1bn and individual partner profit at around £400k per partner (and no debt and very cash flow positive) hesitating about spending around £500k on an investment which their prospective clients are saying is the item that most influences their initial selection.

What they had not realised was just how quickly online information and presentation had become engrained and entrenched and how business habits had changed so fast that the proverbial "tipping point" had been reached. Old fashioned networks and traditional contacts had not been displaced. But they had been added to. And in a material way. Client selection was now "multi-channel" and certainly contained an important digital information component. This had become so vital but the lawyers, immersed in their day-to-day arcane world, had not realised it. They needed the wake-up call!

But this situation is not that untypical. There remains the view that the real B2B activity is still done via a sales force with face to face contact and people who build long term relationships. And nothing wrong with that. But most customers, as the law firm found out, are starting to expect more and more online information. And they expect that to be smartly presented. It's "the face of the firm" to the outside world. They expect extranet facilities where they can check on progress of any joint activities. They expect My Account features so they can look at purchase history, invoice status, payment and receipts. They expect special news updates which are relevant to them and their business. They want content and site material configured for use on their iPad and iPhone, they demand an excellent search facility that lets them find exactly what they want quickly and easily. If Company X is not offering these sort of tools and functions then for sure there's a Company Y knocking on the door with just these sort of initiatives.

★★★★★

A recent "brand health check" carried out by Havas showed that those companies with demonstrated excellence online, the vanguard companies, are still, despite all the case studies, a minority! In their research, spanning over 30,000 people across 4 continents, they found that only 30% of today's largest corporations were considered to have "a meaningful and relevant online presence". And when asked to consider the consequences of that, most of the respondents said that if the company had no engagement online then they would just go to a rival brand or company that did!

So the lessons through all these case studies are clear. An organisation just has to bite the "digital bullet" if it is to truly survive. And that's both with its customers as well as the way it works internally. Let Gartner sum up the challenge:

> *"The digital shift instigated by the nexus of forces (cloud, mobile, social and information) and boosted by "internet of things", threatens many existing businesses. They have no choice but to pursue this".*

Chapter 25

The Age of the Technology Revolution

We are privileged to be living through the "Technology Revolution". In 2050, people will look back on this period with astonishment. They will be amazed at the amount of technology innovation, the pace of it all, the challenges that Businesses had to navigate, the complexity of the changes and yet also the simplicity that it brought. This is a truly a disruptive but exhilarating time.

We are now moving fast into this new era. Digital Tech is impacting the way we communicate, the way we buy things, the way companies interact with customers, the way we talk. Our expectations of what we can do and how we can do it have been transformed. The "i-want-it-now", time poor, technically literate developed world now demands the convenience of being able to do things "my way". Welcome to anytime, anyhow, anywhere!

There's a complete transformation taking place. Technically we've moved at an incredibly rapid pace in past 30 years. We could say we're now in the seventh stage of recent evolution:

Main frame

▼

Mini computers

▼

Desktop

▼

Internet

▼

Mobile
▼
Cloud/ Social
▼
Open Source / ecosystems
▼

The pace of these developments, as observed in a recent Morgan Stanley report, has accelerated. Whether you talk Moore's Law or more simply the billions of dollars of private equity investment, there is a huge amount of continuing R&D and an absolute wealth of ideas and pipeline of new products that are all queuing and lining-up to find their own commercial life-changing, business breakthrough applications.

Where is all this heading? What are we likely to see as the next decade unfolds? Can we even begin to imagine our world post 2020? How soon before computers take control? Here are a few recent headlines:

- "Algorithms take control of Wall Street" (Wired.com)
- "Computer drives car without human control" (Science Daily)
- "Computers to replace teachers" (Daily Telegraph)
- "Technology is taking over the planet" (Helium.com)
- "Computer hardware and software will match the human brain by 2020" (US Robotics Institute)
- "Thinking/learning machines may not be that far away" (NYT/ IBM report)

In the novel "Nine Tomorrows" Isaac Asimov portrays a futuristic world where computers do control humans. Asimov describes how humans become dependent. No need to read books or study. Why bother when the computer already has that knowledge and you can access it when you want? Just rely on computers! Computers start to select from their vast store of knowledge what to teach humans. They make their own priorities and start shaping what humans know. They start to keep some knowledge away from humans and just for their own data banks, for themselves. Computers start to control humans' lives.

Far-fetched? While Asimov is critical of this future dependency, we are already close to it. Google's algorithms decide what we see and in what order we see it. Medical diagnostic software tells physicians what the problem is and what treatment is required. Traffic control systems automatically regulate air traffic and auto routes. Our old-fashioned "Point and Click" world, where we controlled what we would look at is quickly morphing into a two-way "Touch and Talk". We already expect the computer to recognise us. Acknowledge we are a customer, recognise our voice, anticipate our regular commands. If we can talk to our computer then we no longer need a computer screen. We can evolve to "screen-less", interactive, intelligent communication. It can take us into a Stephen Spielberg / Tom Cruise "Minority Report" type world where what 10 years ago was pure science fiction now becomes a reality.

All corporations are now at cross-roads. They can either examine their future and embrace the new digital world. Or they can keep their heads down and hope that its real impact will be delayed. For many companies, their "future strategy" focus is still only looking out at most 12 months. The excuse is: how can we look out any further when the world is changing so rapidly. This short-termism allows execs to develop an incremental holding path where a mix of cost cutting and fighting to maintain customer contracts might just about deliver some kind of acceptable short term budget plan.

But eventually this type of "strategy" is just not going to work. Eventually the new players and rivals will reach critical mass with their new software and approaches. Eventually user / consumer behaviour will change to such a degree that for example a big retailer just will not need all that physical space to display its wares, B2B companies won't need those large salesforces, Marketing departments will no longer be able to justify vast multi-million$ ad spends, IT departments will need to be small, agile and embrace the Cloud, the workforce will be mobile, global, yet remote and virtual (who needs all that expensive head office real estate?)…the list of changes is endless. It may happen in 5 years or 10, but the impact of this technology revolution will be felt, it will not go away or lessen. And so that cross-roads is here. And companies need to decide what to do about it.